The Ultimate University Ranking Guide

trotman

The Ultimate University Ranking Guide

rine Harris

The Ultimate University Ranking Guide
This first edition published in 2004 by Trotman and Company Ltd
2 The Green, Richmond, Surrey TW9 1PL

Reprinted 2005

Editorial and Publishing Team

Author Catherine Harris
Editorial Mina Patria, Editorial Director; Rachel Lockhart, Commissioning
Editor; Catherine Travers, Managing Editor; Bianca Knights, Assistant Editor
Production Ken Ruskin, Head of Pre-press and Production; James Rudge,
Production Artworker
Sales and Marketing Deborah Jones, Head of Sales and Marketing
Advertising Tom Lee, Commercial Director
Managing Director Toby Trotman

Design by Pink Frog

British Library Cataloguing in Publication Data
A catalogue record for this book is available from the British Library

ISBN 0 85660 983 8

Typeset by Avocet Typeset, Chilton, Aylesbury, Bucks
Printed and bound in Great Britain by The Cromwell Press, Trowbridge, Wiltshire

Contents

About the Author

Catherine Harris is a freelance journalist. She studied at Edinburgh University and has written for national and local newspapers, including the *Guardian*, the *Evening Standard* and the *Sunday Mirror*. She has also worked as a researcher in TV and radio at the BBC and in independent production companies. *The Ultimate University Ranking Guide* is her fourth book.

Acknowledgements

I would like to say a huge thank you to all the experts and authors who allowed us to reproduce their work. And thanks to the many students who have contributed greatly to this book. Finally, thank you to everyone at Trotman who has worked so hard to edit and produce *The Ultimate University Ranking Guide*, particularly Rachel Lockhart and Bianca Knights.

Tables on pages 31–33, 36–38, 57–58 and 74 derived from the *Student Book 2005*. Information in the *Student Book* is intended to provide broad brush indicators for potential students and is obtained from a variety of university sources. It is not collected with a view to setting in league tables.

Tables on pages 30–37, 54–55 and 73 from *The Times Good University Guide 2005*, edited by John O'Leary reprinted by permission of HarperCollins Publishers Ltd. Compilation copyright © HarperCollins Publishers 2004.

Accommodation data on pages 78–87 by kind permission of UCAS.

Information for tables on pages 77 and 88 from *Students' Money Matters 2004* by kind permission of Gwenda Thomas.

Virgin subject rankings on pages 14 to 29 are taken from *The Virgin 2005 Alternative Guide to British Universities*, by © Piers Dudgeon 2004, Virgin Books Ltd.

Statistics on page 55–56 from 'Location, Location, Orientation' by Julie Bindel – The *Guardian Weekend*, 27 March 2004, copyright © the *Guardian*.

The Tompkins Table 2004 on page 40 is reproduced with kind permission of Peter Tompkins.

Introduction

University is a place to develop your interests, make lifelong friends and achieve your goals. Pick the right university and your student days could be fantastic fun and academically rewarding.

But choosing a university is a hard decision. With approximately 100 UK universities and around 100 other higher education institutions, the choice can be overwhelming. Researching thoroughly will make your decision easier. A good approach is to select a university with the same care as you would if you were about to buy something very expensive. Because that's exactly what you are about to do. You want value for money, and you want to secure a place on the best possible course at the best possible university for you that your grades allow.

This book is a fantastic place to start your research and to get you thinking about all the factors involved in making your university choice. We've brought together highlights from some of the most informative university rankings out there. With everything from the top universities and best teaching to the cheapest beer and university sporting champions, the university rankings in this guide should inspire you to think about the full university experience, and will point you to other sources so you can continue your research. We think you will get the clearest picture if you research more than one source. That's what this book is all about: encouraging you to look at a range of sources in your own ultimate university research.

We've also done some of our own extensive original research. To find out what life is like at a range of UK universities, we talked to the people who really know – students and ex-students. They've told us about their experiences, including what they wish they'd known before going to university. And that's not all. We've scoured the UK, from Glasgow to Exeter, to ask a selection of student unions about life at their universities. With input from over 60 universities and higher education colleges, our student union ratings will get you thinking about the different opportunities on offer at the UK's universities, and will hopefully inspire you to think of the questions you would like to ask when doing your own research.

With tips and stories from students and recent graduates about how to choose a university and what to get involved in, in no time at all, this book should get you thinking like a student too.

Choosing a university

Choosing a university is all about finding the right balance between the course and the university itself. Once you've decided what course you want to study, you can get an idea which universities are strong in that course by researching league tables. These should be used as a general guide only, as there is some flexibility in how different publications rank universities and courses.

In this book we use highlights from the Virgin subject tables from *The Virgin 2005 Alternative Guide to British Universities*, but also check out the subject tables in other guides such as *The Times Good University Guide 2005* and *The Guardian University Guide 2004*.

It's key to research how courses are taught. For example, one course may place more emphasis on theory, while another may be more practically based. One may take three years, and another four. If you're the type of person who panics in exams, you might want to find a course in which the majority of your final mark is decided by continuous assessment.

The information about courses should be balanced against the type of university you want to go to. For example, do you want to be part of a campus-based university with a strong community feel? Do you want to be near home, or as far away as you can get? This book will give you lots more ideas of the type of considerations that will help you choose the right university and course for you.

Overall academic rankings for each university can be found in league tables such as those produced by *The Times* and the *Guardian*. Do take these rankings into account, but be aware that some universities complain that the rankings are not representative. For example, Edinburgh University, ranked in the mid teens in 2003 by the *FT*, the *Guardian*, the *Sunday Times* and *The Times*, was ranked 42nd in 2003 by the *Daily Telegraph*. Researching as many different sources as possible will also give you a more complete picture. We've used loads of different sources for this book in order to give you an overall view of some of the best information available. That's why we think it's the ultimate starting point for your university research. Remember: once you've narrowed down your university choices, open days are fantastic for getting a sense of the university, and will help you make a much more informed decision.

CHAPTER ONE

Ultimate You

How to choose a university

In the recent *UNITE Student Living Report 2004*, students across the country were asked why they chose their university and this is what they said:

Top reasons why students choose a university

1. The course offered
2. Academic reputation
3. Visited it and liked it
4. Located in city
5. University league tables
6. The atmosphere
7. Ability to live at home
8. Close to my family

| **SOURCE:** *UNITE Student Living Report 2004* |

Your university checklist

You may pick your university for much the same reasons as above or there may be other personal factors that inform your choice.

Get a piece of paper and write down why you want to go to university and what you hope to get out of it. Then get a new piece of paper and make a list of what it is you need to find out in order to achieve your aims. This second list is your university checklist.

As you read this book, add to your checklist. Your list could look something like this:

Sample university checklist

I'm looking for:

1. **A well-respected course with emphasis on practical application**
2. **Good academic reputation of course and university**
3. **Located in city**
4. **Culturally diverse**
5. **Good nightlife**
6. **Community atmosphere**
7. **Active student union**
8. **Good employment prospects on graduation**
9. **Affordability**
10. **Good gym facilities**

We've interviewed loads of students about picking a university, to help give you some ideas.

TOP TIPS

'Research the reputation of the course versus the university. When making a choice of university consider your course, not just the university – even in a good university, a specific department can be quite bad.'
Student from the University of Sussex.

'Find out what's cracking off: the social life, student nights, balls, sports teams and activities available.'
Students from Derby, Portsmouth, Edge Hill College, Liverpool John Moores, University of Wales, Bangor, and Belfast Queen's.

'Check out the local entertainment scene: clubs, music venues, etc.'
Student from De Montfort University.

'Check out the accommodation.'
Students from University College Northampton (UCN) and Exeter.

'Spend time researching, and look at the league tables in the guides and newspapers.'
Student from Bournemouth University.

'I wish I'd thought about employability ratings when I chose a university. But I was lucky as this university does well in employability ratings.'
Student from the University of Central Lancashire (UCLAN).

'Make sure you visit a city university and a campus university as the two are very different – find out which type suits your needs.'
Student from the University of Newcastle.

'Ask if the university has a good active student union.'
Students from Surrey, Sheffield University, Royal Holloway, Oxford Brookes, Loughborough and Imperial College.

'Find out what the surrounding area is like'.
Student from Sunderland.

'Go and visit, so you can see if you like the university's atmosphere.'
Students from St Andrews and Glamorgan.

'The open day was the big swinger for me: I could tell Newcastle was a friendly environment.'
Student from Newcastle.

'Visit the campus and get the feel of the place.'
Student from London Metropolitan.

'You've got to live in your university city for three years, so make sure it suits you. Bath fitted me perfectly because it's about the same size as where I come from, and is a beautiful city with fantastic countryside. I know I'd hate London, for example, because it's just too big.'
Student from Bath Spa University College.

'Make sure the university has good facilities,'
Students from the University of Gloucestershire and Abertay Dundee University.

'Find out the cost of living at the university,'
Students from Bradford and Cambridge.

The rankings in the following chapters – some light-hearted, some serious – are there to inspire you to think about the whole university experience and what you want to get out of it. To know which university and course is right for you, you have to work out what you want. So good luck with your research and university career – we hope this book gives you some great ideas to help you achieve your future goals!

RESEARCH, RESEARCH AND, YOU GUESSED IT, MORE RESEARCH ...

For more information on institutions and a wealth of information on applying to university and courses available, go to www.ucas.com

To find out about university open days, go to www.opendays.com

For comprehensive university profiles, details of which universities offer which courses, and information on everything from entry requirements to student–staff ratio read the *Student Book 2005* published by Trotman.

For university and course league tables and loads of useful university and course information check out *The Times Good University Guide 2005* and *The Guardian University Guide 2004*. There is also good education information at www.guardian.co.uk and www.timesonline.co.uk

For a more alternative insight, read *The Virgin 2005 Alternative Guide to British Universities* or *The Push Guide to Which University* published by Nelson Thomas.

Don't worry: you don't have to buy all these books – they are available from libraries!

UNIVERSITIES ONLINE

Log on to individual university websites for further information and alternative prospectus. (See listings of university websites on page 112).

TOP TIP

'LOOK FOR SOMEWHERE YOU THINK YOU'LL BE COMFORTABLE FOR THREE YEARS. I GOT A GOOD FEELING WHEN I CAME TO LOOK AROUND HERE AND I WAS RIGHT.'

Student from Liverpool John Moores University.

CHAPTER TWO

Ultimate Academia

This chapter gives you selected highlights from academic rankings of universities and courses. All information is sourced, so there are leads for you to follow up if you want to continue your research.

Do our quiz below and start considering a few of the academic factors involved in making your university choice.

Choosing a university

Which one of the following is you?

1) *It's vital that I go to a university with the best academic reputation.*

2) *I want to go somewhere where I can work hard and feel comfortable.*

3) *I want to study somewhere near home so I can work part-time.*

If you picked number one, then you need to find out which universities and courses have the best academic reputation (see below for more information). If you picked number two, you can find out more about lifestyle at different universities on page 41. If you picked number three, you can find out more about choosing the right course on page 11.

Which one of the following is you?

1) *I'm not expecting to do that well in my A-levels or Highers, but I still want to go to university.*

2) *I'm expecting to do well in my A-levels or Highers.*

3) *I'm expecting to do OK in my A-levels or Highers.*

UK universities have a broad range of entry requirements. Go to our lists of universities that require the highest and lowest UCAS points on page 31 to find out more.

Which one of the following is you?

1) *If I'm going to have to borrow all this money to get my degree I want to make sure I can get a good job afterwards.*

2) *I'm just doing my degree for the love of it — I'll think about jobs later.*

3) *I want to work while I do my degree.*

With student debt a consideration, job prospects are increasingly a major factor in any prospective student's decision. Go to page 72 and read our chapter on jobs and money.

The right university

Finding the right university for you means locating a university with the right course, environment and academic challenge to suit your requirements. Academic rankings are an important part of your decision, but it's also important to find somewhere you will feel comfortable, so you will finish your course.

Detailed university profiles can be found in *The Virgin 2005 Alternative Guide to British Universities* and the *Student Book 2005*. Academic rankings for around one hundred key institutions can be found in *The Times University Guide 2005* and *The Guardian University Guide 2004*. These rankings are based on a range of factors, from the institution's teaching score to the student–to–staff ratio and entry requirements. The tables are a useful source of information, but most guides will encourage you to use league tables as a benchmark only.

Indeed some universities strongly contest these academic rankings. In particular, Scottish universities believe they fall foul of the assessment system used by current university league tables. A spokesman from St Andrews was reported in the *Scotsman* to say:

> *'The tables don't take account of research exercise data, which is like trying to rank Celtic without taking account of Henrik Larsson.'*

John Clare, education expert at the *Daily Telegraph*, gives the following general advice about academic university rankings:

> *'League tables as currently constituted are, at best, an imprecise guide. The three universities that undoubtedly enhance a graduate's job prospects are Cambridge, Oxford and Imperial.*

Another 17 are academically selective and generally seen as having high status. Ranked by the value of their research funding, they are: University College London, Edinburgh, King's College London, Manchester, Glasgow, Southampton, Leeds, Birmingham, Sheffield, Nottingham, Bristol, Liverpool, Newcastle, Cardiff, Dundee, Warwick and Leicester. All but Dundee and Leicester are members of the highly regarded Russell Group (www.russellgroup.ac.uk).

'In much the same league, based on the quality of their teaching and research, are LSE, York and Durham. Not far behind are Bath, Loughborough, St Andrews, Lancaster, Exeter and Reading. Aston and Surrey contest the 30th spot.

'The remaining 70 institutions fall into two equal halves: those whose influence on their graduates' job prospects is probably neutral, and those – overwhelmingly the former polytechnics – which, outside certain specialist areas, are widely seen as having low status and likely, therefore, to have a negative impact on their graduates' prospects. They also admit the largest proportion of students through clearing, and have the highest drop-out rates.'

You don't have to go to one of John Clare's high status universities in order to profit from some of the best teaching in the country. Many of the former polytechnics excel academically in specific subjects, so for Building Studies, for example, the *Guardian* rates the Building Studies course at Kingston University as the best course in the country – while Kingston University does not feature in John Clare's list of high status universities.

Premier league

1. **University of Cambridge**

2. **University of Oxford**

3. **Imperial College London**

First Division

4. **University College London**

5. **University of Edinburgh**

6. **King's College London**

7. **University of Manchester**

8. **University of Glasgow**

9. **University of Southampton**

10. **University of Leeds**

11. **University of Birmingham**

12. **University of Sheffield**

13. **University of Nottingham**

14. **University of Bristol**

15. **University of Liverpool**

16. **University of Newcastle**

17. **Cardiff University**

18. **University of Dundee**

19. **University of Warwick**

20. **University of Leicester**

21. **London School of Economics and Political Science**

22. **University of York**

23. **University of Durham**

24. **University of Bath**

25. **Loughborough University**

26. **University of St Andrews**

27. **University of Lancaster**

28. **University of Exeter**

29. **University of Reading**

30. **{University of Aston**

     {University of Surrey

| **SOURCE:** John Clare, *Daily Telegraph*, 18 August 2004 |

The right course

Choosing the right course is essential to your university experience. A course that interests you and helps you achieve your goals will go a long way to making your time at university fun and rewarding. With around 50,000 courses according to UCAS – everything from food science to agriculture and forestry – there should be something for everyone.

Try our quiz below to give you some ideas about choosing a course.

Choosing a course

Which one of the following is you?

1) *I've chosen my subject because it fascinates me.*

2) *I've chosen my subject because I think I will get a good job at the end of it.*

3) *I've chosen my subject because it's got low entry requirements.*

With so many fascinating courses to choose from, picking the right course can be a difficult task. Whatever subject you choose, you will study it for three or four years, so you will obviously enjoy it much more if it interests you. Of course, employability at the end of the course is also a factor for most people. Go to page 73 to see which courses are the worst and best for graduate employability. As regards entry requirements, courses such as veterinary science or medicine require good A-levels, while some other courses are less academically selective. Go to page 30 to see the list of easiest and hardest subjects to get into.

Which one of the following is you?

1) *I've chosen my subject but I haven't found out anything about the different courses on offer. I'm sure they are all pretty much the same.*

2) *I don't care about the type of course – I just want to go to university to have some fun.*

3) *I'm fascinated by my subject and have started researching the different courses: I want to find the one with the best opportunities to develop my interests and achieve my goals.*

If you chose number three, you've got a good chance of finding the right course. If you chose number one or two you're leaving it up to chance. The top reason that people drop out of university, according to the *UNITE Student Living Report 2004*, is that the course wasn't what they expected or wanted. It's essential to work out what you want from a course and why you want to do it, before you apply. Knowing what you want when you research courses will help you to ask the right questions so you can eliminate courses that don't suit your needs before you apply.

For more information on courses, entry requirements and the new UCAS tariff go to www.UCAS.com

FASCINATING FACT

You can apply to as many as six universities on your first UCAS application.

WHERE AM I GOING?

Not everyone has chosen a career before they go to university. If you are one of the lucky ones and have already worked it out, get some advice about the best course for your chosen career. The Prospects website at www.prospects.ac.uk – the official graduate careers website – is packed with detailed information on careers and relevant degree courses. Knowing why you want to do a particular course could help you in the application process and will aid motivation during your degree. If you have chosen a subject simply because you enjoy it, that in itself is a very good reason to go to university. However, speaking to a careers adviser and visiting a site like the Prospects site can help you start thinking about your future.

Once you've narrowed down the type of course you want to do, then you need to research the individual courses and start asking questions. How long is the course? How practical or theoretical? Does it include a year abroad or in a relevant business environment? What are the entry requirements? There is a wealth of useful information on the UCAS website at www.ucas.com, including what subjects and grades are needed for specific courses. Even in the same subject, entry grades will differ between courses.

Research a range of university guides to find out more information about your course at different universities. The *Virgin Guide* subject rankings (highlights printed below) place courses in each university in high, medium and low bands according to entry requirements. *The Guardian University Guide 2004* and *The Times Good University Guide 2005* offer a ranking system from number one down. In some cases there is a difference of opinion about the top ranking courses – that's why it's useful to research more than one source to get an overall picture. In nursing, for example, the *Guardian* places Plymouth University, Sunderland University and University of Wales, Swansea, as the top three while *The Times* places Manchester, Northumbria and Portsmouth as the top three universities for nursing. Both guides give a detailed description of how they assess the courses, providing extremely valuable information, including teaching scores and job prospects. Using all this information, you can start to make up your own mind about which you think is the best course for you.

Now you've researched the guides, send off for prospectuses from universities and research university websites. Most university departments provide detailed information about courses on their websites. For university web addresses go to page 117.

Try and speak to someone who is doing, or has done, the course you are interested in – there's nothing as revealing as first-hand knowledge. And make use of open days to research your course and department further.

'I wish I'd considered the reputation of my course a little harder. When I heard what Margaret Hodge had to say about Mickey-Mouse courses, I felt really disheartened. Also a senior person in the BBC came to talk to us and said an undergraduate media degree made no difference in terms of getting a job at the BBC. However, I've really enjoyed my course and feel I've learnt valuable skills.' – Third-year Media Studies undergraduate.

'I'm so pleased I chose to do law at Queen's. The standard of teaching and the quality of the lectures was high – there's also a good social life in the law society.' – Student who graduated with a law degree from Queen's University Belfast in 2004.

'I really enjoyed my third year when I chose my options. That meant I could pick the subjects that interested me, that were taught by people who were passionate about their subject. Although I didn't really enjoy the first two years of my course, I had fun at Warwick and enjoyed my time as a student. It does have a good reputation, and the fact that I've got a 2:1 from Warwick will open doors for me.' – 2003 Psychology graduate from Warwick.

'For my course I did a four-year teaching degree in PE. It's the only course in the country and it's got an A from Ofsted. I found it an excellent course.' – Recent graduate from Liverpool John Moores University.

'I wish I'd known that the Performing Arts course was not what I had imagined from the description in the prospectus.' – Student from De Montfort University.

'Modern universities like UEL offer untraditional courses – the courses here have been recently set up, so subjects such as media, film, fashion, graphics and design are up to speed with modern interests.' – Student from University of East London.

Virgin subject rankings

(For comprehensive listings of all universities and all subjects read *The Virgin 2005 Alternative Guide to British Universities*, *The Guardian University Guide 2004* and *The Times University Guide 2004*. You could also check out *Choosing Your Degree Course and University* by Brian Heap).

In the following tables, Column 1 shows the official entry levels. To convert A-levels to points use the following key:

A = 120 points

B = 100 points

C = 80 points

D = 60 points

E = 40 points

Column three shows the teaching ratings by outside inspectors. These have been compiled by the QAA and Higher Education Funding Councils for England and Wales. Where points are awarded, they are out of 24. Where a word is used, English and Welsh universities are graded from three choices: Excellent, Satisfactory and Unsatisfactory, while Scottish universities are assessed as Excellent, Highly Satisfactory, Satisfactory or Unsatisfactory.

Table 2.1 Virgin subject rankings

Accountancy/Finance		
Entry	Uni/College	Rating
High		Economics/Maths
280 points +	University of Manchester Institute of Science and Technology	–/22
	University of Warwick	24/22
	University of Edinburgh	Excellent
	London School of Economics and Political Science	23/22
	University of Nottingham	24/23
	Queen's University Belfast	24/22
	Aston University	–/19
	University of Birmingham	23/24
	University of Wales, Swansea	
	University of Sheffield	21/21
	University of Leeds	22/22
	University of Manchester	24/22
	University of Newcastle Upon Tyne	23/23
	University of Glasgow	Highly Satisfactory
	Cardiff University	Excellent
	City University	22/23
	University of East Anglia	23/23
	Lancaster University	–/22
	University of Bristol	23/23
	University of Reading	22/21
	University of Exeter	22/22
	University of Southampton	24/20
Agriculture, Forestry, Agricultural Sciences		
Entry	Uni/College	Rating
Medium–high		
240–280 points	University of Birmingham	
	University of Sussex	
	University of Leeds	20
	University of Kent	
	University of Glasgow	
American Studies		
Entry	Uni/College	Rating
High		
280 points +	University of Birmingham	22
	University of Edinburgh	
	University of Hull	23
	University of Nottingham	22

American Studies

Entry	Uni/College	Rating
	University of Sheffield	
	University of Sussex	23
	University of Wales, Swansea	Satisfactory
	University of Warwick	

Archaeology

Entry	Uni/College	Rating
High		
280 points +	University of Cambridge	23
	University of Oxford	22
	University of St Andrews	
	University of Sheffield	22
	University College London	23
	University of Birmingham	22
	University of York	24
	King's College London	
	University of East Anglia	

Architecture/Design/Eng.

Entry	Uni/College	Rating
High		
280 points +	University of Cambridge	Excellent
	University of Edinburgh	Highly Satisfactory
	University of Newcastle Upon Tyne	Excellent
	University of Liverpool	Satisfactory
	University of Nottingham	Excellent
	University of Sheffield	Excellent
	University of Bath	Excellent
	Cardiff University	Excellent
	University of Strathclyde	Excellent
	University College London	Excellent
	Kingston University	Satisfactory

Art: Fine Art/Illustration

Entry	Uni/College	Rating
High		
280 points +	University of Oxford	24
	University of Exeter	
	University of Leeds	23
Medium-high		
240 – 280 points	University of Wales, Aberystwyth	Satisfactory
	University of Central England	22
	University of Derby	20

Art: Fine Art/Illustration

Entry	Uni/College	Rating
	University of Newcastle Upon Tyne	20
	Northumbria University	22
	Nottingham Trent University	22

Biosciences

Entry	Uni/College	Rating*
High		
280 points +	University of Bath	24
	University of Birmingham	24, 23
	University of Bristol	22, 24
	University of Cambridge	24
	Cardiff University	Excellent
	University of Edinburgh	Excellent
	University of Exeter	22
	University of Hull	23
	Imperial College London	22
	University of Kent	24
	King's College London	22
	University of Leeds	22, 23
	University of Manchester	23
	University of Manchester Institute of Science and Technology	22
	University of Nottingham	23
	University of Oxford	24
	Queen Mary, University of London	22
	University of Southampton	23
	University of Wales, Swansea	Excellent
	University College London	24, 22

Business Management

Entry	Uni/College	Rating
High		
280 points +	University of Bath	
	University of Birmingham	21
	University of Bristol	
	Brunel University	
	Cardiff University	
	City University	23
	University of Durham	
	University of Edinburgh	
	Imperial College London	

*Assessments have been made for both molecular and organismal biosciences; where the outcome was different in each case, the first of the two scores in column 3 relates to organismal biosciences.

Business Management

Entry	Uni/College	Rating
	Keele University	21
	King's College London	
	Lancaster University	
	University of Leeds	22
	London School of Economics and Political Science	24
	Loughborough University	22
	University of Newcastle Upon Tyne	
	University of Nottingham	
	University of Oxford	
	University of Reading	21
	Royal Holloway, University of London	21
	University of St Andrews	
	School of Oriental and African Studies	
	University of Sheffield	
	University of Southampton	
	University of Surrey	23
	University College London	
	University of Warwick	
	University of York	22

Chemistry

Entry	Uni/College	Rating
High		
280 points +	University of Birmingham	Satisfactory
	University of Cambridge	Excellent
	University of Durham	Excellent
	University of Glasgow	Excellent
	Imperial College London	Excellent
	King's College London	Satisfactory
	University of Oxford	Excellent
	University of Southampton	Excellent
	University of York	Satisfactory

Computer

Entry	Uni/College	Rating
High		
280 points +	University of Cambridge	Excellent
	University of Oxford	Excellent
	Imperial College London	Excellent
	University of Bristol	Satisfactory
	University of York	Excellent

Computer

Entry	Uni/College	Rating
	University College London	Satisfactory
	University of Manchester	Excellent
	University of Warwick	Excellent
	University of Southampton	Excellent
	King's College London	Satisfactory
	Royal Holloway, University of London	Satisfactory
	University of Leeds	Satisfactory
	University of Durham	Satisfactory

Dentistry

Entry	Uni/College	Rating
High		
280 points +	University of Bristol	19
	Queen's University Belfast	24
	University of Liverpool	21
	University of Birmingham	22
	University of Dundee	Highly Satisfactory
	University of Glasgow	Highly Satisfactory
	King's College London	24
	University of Leeds	23
	University of Manchester	24
	University of Newcastle Upon Tyne	23
	Queen Mary, University of London	24
	University of Sheffield	23
	University of Wales College of Medicine	

Drama/Theatre Arts

Entry	Uni/College	Rating
High		
280 points +	University of Cambridge	
	University of Leeds	
	University of Birmingham	21
	University of East Anglia	21
	University of Manchester	21
	Royal Holloway, University of London	23
	University of Reading	24
	University of Sussex	
	University of Warwick	24
	University of Exeter	22
	Lancaster University	24
	University of Glasgow	Highly Satisfactory

Drama/Theatre Arts

Entry	Uni/College	Rating
	Goldsmiths College	22
	Queen Mary and Westfield College, University of London	21
	University of Kent	24

Economics

Entry	Uni/College	Rating
High		
280 points +	University of Cambridge	24
	University of Oxford	23
	University of Warwick	24
	London School of Economics and Political Science	23
	University of Nottingham	24
	University of Durham	24
	University College London	24
	University of Edinburgh	Satisfactory
	Aston University	
	University of Bath	24
	University of Sussex	21
	University of St Andrews	Excellent
	University of Bristol	23
	University of Manchester	24
	University of Birmingham	23
	University of Glasgow	Satisfactory
	University of Leeds	22
	University of Sheffield	21
	University of Southampton	24
	University of Essex	24

Engineering (General)

Entry	Uni/College	Rating
High		
280 points +	University of Cambridge	23
	Imperial College London	23
	University of Oxford	23
	University of Bristol	
	University of Dundee	
	University of Durham	22

English

Entry	Uni/College	Rating
High		
280 points +	University of Cambridge	Excellent
	University of Oxford	Excellent

English

Entry	Uni/College	Rating
	University College London	Excellent
	King's College London	Satisfactory
	University of Birmingham	Excellent
	University of Edinburgh	Highly Satisfactory
	University of East Anglia	Satisfactory
	University of Manchester	Satisfactory
	University of St Andrews	Highly Satisfactory
	University of Southampton	Excellent
	University of Sussex	Excellent
	University of Newcastle Upon Tyne	Excellent
	University of Durham	Excellent
	University of Exeter	Excellent
	University of Bristol	Excellent
	University of Leeds	Excellent
	University of Sheffield	Excellent
	University of Warwick	Excellent
	Cardiff University	Excellent
	University of Liverpool	Excellent
	University of York	Excellent
	University of Nottingham	Excellent
	Royal Holloway, University of London	Satisfactory
	University of Glasgow	Excellent
	Lancaster University	Excellent
	University of Wales, Swansea	Satisfactory
	University of Kent	Satisfactory

Geography

Entry	Uni/College	Rating
High		
280 points +	University of Cambridge	Excellent
	University of Oxford	Excellent
	University of Bristol	Excellent
	University of Durham	Excellent
	University of St Andrews	Excellent
	King's College London	Excellent
	University of Sheffield	Excellent
	London School of Economics and Political Science	Satisfactory
	University of Edinburgh	Highly Satisfactory
	University of Nottingham	Excellent
	University College London	Excellent
	University of Reading	Excellent
	University of Liverpool	Satisfactory

History

Entry	Uni/College	Rating
High		
280 points +	University of Cambridge	Excellent
	University of Oxford	Excellent
	London School of Economics and Political Science	Excellent
	Royal Holloway, University of London	Excellent
	University of Edinburgh	Excellent
	University of York	Excellent
	University of St Andrews	Excellent
	University of Southampton	Satisfactory
	University of Warwick	Excellent
	University of Durham	Excellent
	University of Manchester	Satisfactory
	University of Sheffield	Excellent
	University of Glasgow	Highly Satisfactory
	University of Leeds	Satisfactory
	University of Sussex	Satisfactory
	University of Kent	Satisfactory

Languages (French, German)

Entry	Uni/College	Rating
High		
280 points +	University of Cambridge	22
	University of Oxford	21
	British Institute	18
	University of Manchester	19, Fr; 21, Gr
	University of Birmingham	18,Fr; 19, Gr
	University of St Andrews	22
	Royal Holloway, University of London	21, Fr; 19, Gr
	University of Edinburgh	21
	University of Durham	22
	King's College London	21, Fr; 20, Gr
	University of Glasgow	22
	University of Leeds	22, Fr; 22, Gr
	University of Sheffield	21, Fr;20, Gr
	Heriot-Watt University	21
	Slavonic and East European Studies, University College London	
	University of York	22
	University of Southampton	18

Law		
Entry	Uni/College	Rating
High		
280 points+	University of Cambridge	Excellent
	University of Bristol	Excellent
	University of Birmingham	Satisfactory
	University of Edinburgh	Highly Satisfactory
	University of Leeds	Satisfactory
	University of Oxford	Excellent
	University College London	Excellent
	University of Durham	Excellent
	King's College London	Excellent
	University of Manchester	Excellent
	University of Nottingham	Excellent
	Queen's University Belfast	Excellent
	University of Sheffield	Excellent
	University of Warwick	Excellent
	University of Reading	Satisfactory
	University of Glasgow	Highly Satisfactory
	London School of Economics and Political Science	Excellent
	University of Southampton	Satisfactory
	University of Leicester	Excellent
	Cardiff University	Satisfactory
	University of Newcastle Upon Tyne	Satisfactory
	Oxford Brookes University	Excellent
	Queen Mary, University of London	Satisfactory
	Brunel University	Satisfactory
	City University	Satisfactory
	University of East Anglia	Excellent
	University of Sussex	Satisfactory
	School of Oriental and African Studies	Excellent
	University of Liverpool	Excellent
	University of Wales, Swansea	Satisfactory
	University of Wales, Aberystwyth	Satisfactory
	University of Dundee	Highly Satisfactory
	Kingston University	Satisfactory
	Manchester Metropolitan University	Satisfactory
	Nottingham Trent University	Satisfactory
	University of Strathclyde	Highly Satisfactory
	University of Ulster	Satisfactory
	University of Hull	Satisfactory

Mathematics		
Entry	Uni/College	Rating
High		
280 points+	University of Cambridge	23
	University of Oxford	22
	University of Warwick	22
	University of Durham	21
	Imperial College	22
	University of Bristol	23
	London School of Economics and Political Science	22
	University of Birmingham	24
	University of Southampton	20
	Royal Holloway, University of London	22
	University of Edinburgh	Excellent
	University of Manchester	22
	University of Sheffield	21
	University of Nottingham	23
	University of Leeds	22
	University of Bath	24
	University of St Andrews	Excellent
	University of Manchester Institute of Science and Technology	22
	University of Sussex	23
	University of Wales, Swansea	Satisfactory
	Brunel University	22
	Cardiff University	Satisfactory
	University of York	22
	University of Kent	21
	King's College London	21
	University of Liverpool	23
	University of Portsmouth	22
	University of Leicester	22
	Aston University	19
	University of Salford	21
	University College London	23
	University of Exeter	22
	University of Glasgow	Highly Satisfactory
	Queen's University Belfast	22
	University of Newcastle Upon Tyne	23
	University of Essex	20
	University of Surrey	21

Media

Entry	Uni/College	Rating
High		
280 points +	University of Warwick	23
	University of Leeds	22
	University of Sussex	21
	City University	19
	University of Leicester	21
	University of Sheffield	
	University of Birmingham	
	Nottingham Trent University	21
	University of Westminster	23
	University of Liverpool	
	Bournemouth University	22
	Goldsmiths College	22
	Cardiff University	Satisfactory
	Royal Holloway, University of London	
	University of Stirling	Highly Satisfactory
	University of Essex	

Medicine

Entry	Uni/College	Rating
High		
280 points+	University of Cambridge	21
	University of Oxford	21
	University of Birmingham	20
	University of Bristol	20
	University of Edinburgh	Highly Satisfactory
	University of Glasgow	Excellent
	University of Leicester	23
	University of Manchester	24
	University of Newcastle Upon Tyne	24
	University of Nottingham	
	Queen's University Belfast	22
	University of Wales College of Medicine	
	St George's Hospital Medical School	23
	University of Dundee	Excellent
	University College London	21
	(Royal Free	18)
	University of Aberdeen	Excellent
	Imperial College London	21
	King's College London	22
	University of Liverpool	24

Medicine

Entry	Uni/College	Rating
	Queen Mary and Westfield College, University of London	21
	University of Sheffield	19
	University of Southampton	24
	University of St Andrews	Highly Satisfactory
	University of Leeds	18

Music

Entry	Uni/College	Rating
High		
280 points +	University of Cambridge	Excellent
	King's College London	Excellent
	University of Birmingham	Excellent
	University of Oxford	Satisfactory
	Imperial College London	
	University of Nottingham	Excellent
	Royal Academy	Excellent
	University of Manchester	Excellent
	University of Glasgow	Highly Satisfactory
	Royal Holloway, University of London	Satisfactory
	Goldsmiths College	Excellent
	University of Sussex	Excellent
	University of York	Excellent
	University of Southampton	Excellent
	University of Bristol	Satisfactory
	University of Liverpool	Satisfactory
	University of Sheffield	Excellent

Physics

Entry	Uni/College	Rating
High		
280 points +	University of Cambridge	23
	University of Oxford	23
	Imperial College	22
	University of Bristol	23
	University of Warwick	24
	University of Durham	24
	Royal Holloway, University of London	23
	University of Nottingham	23
	Liverpool John Moores University	

Politics		
Entry	Uni/College	Rating
High		
280 points +	University of Cambridge	23
	University of Oxford	24
	University of St Andrews	
	London School of Economics and Political Science	22
	University of Newcastle Upon Tyne	23
	University of Edinburgh	Highly Satisfactory
	University of Nottingham	24
	Royal Holloway, University of London	
	University of Warwick	24
	University of Bristol	23
	University of Durham	21
	University of Exeter	23
	University of Liverpool	
	University of Manchester	24
	University of Birmingham	24
	University of Leeds	23
	University of Sheffield	24
	University of Sussex	23
	University of East Anglia	24
	University of Glasgow	Highly Satisfactory
	University of Reading	22
	University of Bath	24

Psychology		
Entry	Uni/College	Rating
High		
280 points+	University of Cambridge	24
	University of Oxford	24
	University of Durham	23
	University of Edinburgh	Highly Satisfactory
	University of Leeds	23
	University of Sheffield	22
	University College London	22
	University of St Andrews	Excellent
	University of Bath	
	University of Nottingham	24
	University of Birmingham	23
	University of Liverpool	22
	University of Warwick	21
	University of York	24
	University of Bristol	23

Psychology

Entry	Uni/College	Rating
	Cardiff University	Excellent
	London School of Economics and Political Science	23
	Royal Holloway, University of London	24
	University of Sussex	21
	University of Kent	22
	University of Newcastle Upon Tyne	24
	University of Manchester	22
	University of Hull	23
	University of Reading	24
	University of Wales, Swansea	Excellent
	City University	21
	Goldsmiths College	22
	Queen's University Belfast	24
	University of Surrey	22
	Loughborough University	24
	University of Essex	22

Social Policy

Entry	Uni/College	Rating
High		
280 points +	University of Edinburgh	Excellent
	London School of Economics and Political Science	Excellent
	Royal Holloway, University of London	
	University of Glasgow	Excellent
	University of Nottingham	21
	University of Sheffield	Excellent
	University of Sussex	Satisfactory
	University of Essex	

Sociology

Entry	Uni/College	Rating
High		
280 points +	University of Cambridge	
	University of Oxford	
	University of Edinburgh	Excellent
	University of Bristol	21
	Royal Holloway, University of London	21
	Aston University	
	London School of Economics and Political Science	20

Sociology

Entry	Uni/College	Rating
	University of Manchester	21
	University of Leeds	20
	University of Birmingham	24
	University of East Anglia	16
	University of Glasgow	Excellent
	University of Nottingham	21
	University of Sheffield	Excellent
	University of Surrey	21
	University of Sussex	24
	University of Essex	22

Sport/Science

Entry	Uni/College	Rating
High		
280 points +	University of Bath	23
	University of Birmingham	22
	University of Leeds	
	University of Stirling	
	University of Ulster	

Theology

Entry	Uni/College	Rating
High		
280 points +	University of Cambridge	23
	University of Oxford	23
	University of Birmingham	23
	University of Edinburgh	Highly Satisfactory

Veterinary Science

Entry	Uni/College	Rating
High		
280 points +	University of Cambridge	23
	Royal Veterinary College	24
	University of Edinburgh	Excellent
	University of Glasgow	Excellent
	University of Liverpool	24

TOP TIP

'CHECK TO ENSURE ANY COURSE YOU DO IS
APPROVED BY A PROFESSIONAL BODY. IF IT
ISN'T, IT MIGHT NOT BE WORTH AS MUCH.'
– STUDENT FROM LONDON METROPOLITAN
UNIVERSITY.

WANT TO SPEND SOME TIME ABROAD DURING YOUR COURSE?

If a year out during your course in a European Union country sounds appealing,
then find out more about the UK Socrates–Erasmus Council at
www.erasmus.ac.uk

Top ten hardest subjects to get into

1. Veterinary Science
2. Medicine
3. Dentistry
4. Ophthalmics
5. Mathematics
6. Physics
7. Classics
8. Philosophy
9. French
10. Chemical Engineering

| **SOURCE:** *The Times Good University Guide 2005*/HESA |

Top ten easiest subjects to get into

1. Social Work
2. Catering and Institutional Management
3. Building
4. Environmental Technologies
5. Teacher Training
6. Industrial Relations
7. Physical Education
8. Media Studies
9. Food Science
10. Design Studies

| **SOURCE:** *The Times Good University Guide 2005*/HESA |

WANT TO FOLLOW IN FAMOUS FOOTSTEPS?

Check out our famous alumni on page 90.

Other useful academia-related rankings

Average UCAS points on entry – highest

1. University of Nottingham	421
2. University of York	417+
3. University of Cambridge	360+
4. London School of Economics and Political Science	360
5. {University of Oxford	350+
{Royal Veterinary College	350+
6. Imperial College London	340+

7. **Saint George's Hospital Medical School, University of London** — **335+**

8. **University of Bristol** — **330+**

| SOURCE: *Student Book 2005*, Klaus Boehm and Jenny Lees-Spalding, Trotman |

Average UCAS points – lowest (of those that require UCAS points)

1. **Myerscough College** — **80**
2. **Laban Centre** — **120**
3. **Writtle College** — **140**
4. **Trinity College Carmarthen** — **140+**
5. **Buckinghamshire Chilterns University College** — **160**
   {Bolton Institute — **160**
   {Royal Agricultural College — **160**
   {St Mary's College — **160**
   {Southampton Institute — **160**
   {Surrey Institute — **160**

| SOURCE: *Student Book 2005*, Klaus Boehm and Jenny Lees-Spalding, Trotman |

Top ten for teaching quality

1. **University of York**
2. **University of Cambridge**
3. **Loughborough University**
4. **University of St Andrews**
5. **University of Warwick**
6. **University of Essex**
7. **University of Wales, Lampeter**
8. **University of Dundee**
9. **University of Oxford**
10. **University of Glasgow**

| SOURCE: *The Times Good University Guide 2005* |

Bottom ten for teaching quality (best to worst)

1. Anglia Polytechnic University
2. University of Teesside
3. University of Wales, Newport
4. Leeds Metropolitan University
5. University of Central England
6. London South Bank University
7. University of Derby
8. Thames Valley University
9. University of Bournemouth
10. University of East London

| **SOURCE:** *The Times Good University Guide 2005*/HESA |

Highest drop-out rate

1. London South Bank University	21%
2. Bolton Institute	19%
3. {London Metropolitan University	18%
{Paisley University	18%
5. Thames Valley University	17%
{Greenwich University	16%
{Lampeter University	16%
8. {Abertay Dundee University	15%
{Napier University	15%

| **SOURCE:** *Student Book 2005*, Klaus Boehm and Jenny Lees-Spalding,Trotman |

Lowest drop-out rate

1. {University of Cambridge	1%
{University College London	1%
{University of Oxford	1%

4. {University of Bristol	2%
{University of Nottingham	2%
{Imperial College	2%
7. {University of Durham	3%
{Northern School of Contemporary Dance	3%
{Royal College of Music	3%
{Royal Veterinary College	3%

| SOURCE: *Student Book 2005*, Klaus Boehm and Jenny Lees-Spalding, Trotman |

Top five reasons for dropping out

1. Course was not what I expected/wanted
2. Financial problems
3. Lack of support from university
4. Course too difficult
5. Feeling isolated and lonely

| SOURCE: *UNITE Student Living Report 2004* |

Top ten for library/computer spending

1. University of Oxford
2. University of Abertay Dundee
3. School of Oriental and African Studies (SOAS)
4. London School of Economics and Political Science (LSE)
5. University College London
6. University of Cambridge
7. Imperial College London
8. University of Edinburgh
9. King's College London
10. University of Manchester

| SOURCE: *The Times Good University Guide 2005*/HESA |

Bottom ten for library/computer spending (best to worst)

1. Napier University

2. University of the Arts, London

3. University of Salford

4. London South Bank University

5. University of Teesside

6. University of Gloucestershire

7. University of Wales, Newport

8. University of Huddersfield

9. Anglia Polytechnic University

10. Glasgow Caledonian University

| SOURCE: *The Times Good University Guide 2005*/HESA |

I WISH I'D KNOWN . . .

... that Aston University is like a family and how busy my social life was going to be. Fitting studying around having fun was a really hard task as there was always somewhere to go and something to do. The problem with living in the Aston family was that whenever you got up to mischief, everyone knew about it by the next day.' – Student from Aston.

Most firsts and upper seconds

1. University of Cambridge	89.3%
2. University of Oxford	86.7%
3. University of Bristol	81.6%
4. University of St Andrews	78.4%
5. University of Warwick	77.8%
6. University of Edinburgh	76.1%
7. University of Nottingham	75.7%
8. School of Oriental and African Studies (SOAS)	75.1%
9. University of Bath	74.8%
10. University of Exeter	74.1%

| SOURCE: *The Times Good University Guide 2005*/HESA |

Fewest firsts and upper seconds

1. University of Teesside	39.3%
2. University of East London	39.5%
3. Thames Valley University	40%
4. University of Huddersfield	44.1%
5. University of West of England	44.3%
6. London South Bank University	44.4%
7. Staffordshire University	44.8%
8. University of Paisley	45.4%
9. Coventry University	45.7%
10. University of Gloucestershire	46.8%

| SOURCE: *The Times Good University Guide 2005*/HESA |

Top 'toff' unis

1. Royal Agricultural College (48% state school entry)
2. {University of Oxford (55% state school entry)
   {University of Cambridge (55% state school entry)
4. Royal Veterinary College (56% state school entry)
5. University College London (58% state school entry)
6. Imperial College London (59% state school entry)
7. University of Bristol (60% state school entry)
8. University of St Andrews (62% state school entry)
9. University of Edinburgh (63% state school entry)
10. London School of Economics and Political Science (LSE)
    (64% state school entry)

| SOURCE: *Student Book 2005*, Klaus Boehm and Jenny Lees-Spalding, Trotman |

I WISH I'D KNOWN . . .

... 'the amount of hills in Aberystwyth' – Student from Aberystwyth.

Top state entry unis

1. {Queen's University Belfast		100%
{University of Ulster		100%
{Bolton Institute		100%
4. {Edge Hill College of Higher Education		99%
{Falmouth College of Arts		99%
{Trinity College Carmarthen		99%
{Surrey Institute		99%
{Norwich School of Art		99%
{Kent Institute		99%
{Wimbledon School of Art		99%

| SOURCE: Tables compiled from data in the *Student Book 2005*, Klaus Boehm and Jenny Lees-Spalding, Trotman. Data compiled from HEFC figures. Information refers to first-degree students in 2001/02 (the latest year for which information is available). |

Most overseas students

- University of the Arts
- University of Middlesex
- University of Manchester
- University College London
- Coventry University
- Westminster University
- University of Edinburgh
- University of Nottingham
- King's College London
- University of Luton

| SOURCE: Tables compiled from data in *The Times Good University Guide 2005*/HESA, including number of EU and non EU students. |

I WISH I'D KNOWN . . .

'Nothing. Before coming to university I had found out almost everything and was happy with it all.' – Student from Abertay Dundee.

Oldest

- **Oxford and Cambridge (12th and 13th Centuries)**
- **Aberdeen, Glasgow, Edinburgh, St Andrews (15th and 16th Centuries)**
- **Some of the older medical schools, now often part of younger universities**

| **SOURCE:** *Student Book 2005*, Klaus Boehm and Jenny Lees-Spalding, Trotman |

Oxbridge

If you are academic, don't rule out Oxford and Cambridge because you think they are elitist. Although they still take a large proportion of their intake from public school (45%), the majority of students come from the state sector. State school entries are up by 2% on last year and are likely to continue rising. Both websites (www.oxford.ac.uk and www.cam.ac.uk) are packed with information on university life and how to apply. Look up their alternative prospectuses at www.ousu.org/main/ProspectiveStudents and www.cusu.cam.ac.uk.

I WISH I'D KNOWN . . .

'... more about how other university courses work – Oxford's teaching system is unique (except for Cambridge), relying on very small groups with one tutor rather than lectures for its main teaching, and your degree rests almost entirely on your final exams. I wish I'd had more to compare that system to before I came. Also, knowing about the difference between the colleges is very helpful – they all have different facilities and atmospheres, and looking round the colleges before applying is advised.' – Student from Oxford University.

If you do decide you want to try for Oxford or Cambridge you will need to pick a college before you apply. Oxford and Cambridge colleges are ranked in the famous Norrington and Tompkins tables. The tables rank colleges by students' final grades. A first is awarded five points, while a third receives one point. The tables are not compiled or endorsed by the universities.

Table 2.2 Oxford – The Norrington Table 2004

Rank 2004	Rank 2003	College	1sts	2.1s	2.2s	3rds	Total %
1	1	Merton	41	40	6	0	77.47
2	6	St John's	38	58	6	0	73.73
3	16	St Catz	39	71	12	1	73.39
4	5	Balliol	35	55	7	0	72.99
5	19	Hertford	36	59	8	1	71.92
6	3	Magdalen	36	65	7	2	71.09
7	13	Jesus	23	57	3	0	70.36
8	2	Wadham	33	74	6	1	70.18
9	20	Teddy Hall	33	73	8	1	69.74
10	18	St Peter's	27	54	10	0	69.67
11	7	New	30	64	8	2	69.23
12	12	Worcester	27	77	6	0	68.73
13	9	Exeter	17	56	3	0	68.16
14	15	Corpus Christi	15	33	6	1	68.00
15	28	Somerville	23	59	10	0	67.83
16	22	Lincoln	17	54	3	1	67.73
17	8	St Anne's	28	82	10	0	67.67
18	17	St Hugh's	26	75	10	1	67.50
19	23	Oriel	17	46	6	1	67.43
20	8	Christ Church	24	80	7	2	66.55
20=	21	Keble	23	82	7	1	66.55
22	25	Pembroke	20	67	7	1	66.53
23	11	Trinity	15	46	7	1	66.09
24	13	Brasenose	16	70	7	0	65.38
25	4	University	26	74	18	6	64.26
26	27	Queen's	17	50	15	2	63.57
27	29	LMH	17	68	13	2	63.40
28	30	Harris Manchester	2	8	2	0	63.33
29	26	Mansfield	8	39	9	0	62.50
30	24	St Hilda's	12	78	9	2	62.18

Table 2.3 Cambridge – The Tompkins Table 2004

Rank 2004	Rank 2003	College	Total %	%Firsts
1	1	Emmanuel	67.95%	31.50%
2	2	Christ's	67.24%	29.70%
3	8	Trinity	66.88%	31.70%
4	6	Clare	65.94%	27.20%
5	4	Gonville and Caius	65.83%	26.10%
6	3	Pembroke	65.44%	27.70%
7	11	St. Catherine's	65.24%	24.30%
8	5	Queens'	64.20%	23.70%
9	10	Jesus	64.18%	24.50%
10	7	Corpus Christi	63.69%	24.10%
11	14	Selwyn	63.57%	22.00%
12	19	Trinity Hall	62.83%	19.80%
13	21	Newnham	62.80%	19.60%
14	13	St John's	62.77%	20.20%
15	20	Fitzwilliam	62.59%	19.80%
16	23	Robinson	62.04%	18.10%
17	12	Downing	61.53%	17.60%
18	15	Sidney Sussex	61.01%	17.40%
19	9	Churchill	60.92%	20.80%
20	16	King's	60.86%	18.90%
21	22	Peterhouse	60.74%	19.40%
22	18	Magdalene	59.59%	13.70%
23	24	New Hall	58.86%	15.00%
24	25	Homerton	58.73%	10.80%
25	17	Girton	58.67%	13.20%
26	26	Lucy Cavendish	56.55%	7.90%
27	24	Hughes Hall	55.54%	15.60%
28	28	Wolfson	55.36%	13.20%
29	29	St Edmund's	54.45%	15.20%

I WISH I'D KNOWN . . .

'... the intensity of term-time compared to the long holidays.' – Student from Cambridge.

CHAPTER THREE

Ultimate Lifestyle

Your everyday life at university will be influenced by the environment – the people, the campus and the accommodation. The more positively you feel influenced by your environment, the easier it will be to work hard and excel at your course. That's why open days are so important. Alternative prospectuses, mostly to be found online at the university's website, are a fantastic source of information about life as a student at a particular university. Also check out student union websites (see list on page 112) for more insider information.

Do our quiz to get you thinking about student lifestyle.

Student lifestyle

Which one of the following is you?

1) *Aesthetics mean everything to me. There's nothing more depressing than grey concrete.*

2) *I'm not too bothered about my surroundings as long as there's a kicking nightlife.*

3) *I just want practicality: a place where I can get from A to B with no fuss.*

We keep saying it, but we're going to say it again. Open days are a must so you can get a feel of a place. The hundreds of universities and higher education colleges across the UK have some very different looks and atmospheres. Edinburgh, for example, is a mix of traditional and modern, with university buildings spread out across the city, while the University of East Anglia is a modern sixties' campus university, with all its buildings in one central space. Here's an example of how the wrong environment can affect your studies: although the majority of students love Manchester University, one student told me she found the environment at Manchester so depressing that she spent as much time as possible going back home to Bath – and all the travelling is affecting her studies. Check out our student union survey below to see how students rated their university for attractiveness.

Which one of the following is you?

  1) *I love getting involved. I want to be part of the union and help organise lots of fun stuff for other students and myself.*

  2) *I'm not interested in any of that group activity stuff – it bores me.*

  3) *I'd rather sort out my own good times.*

Unions are about more than organising rag week. Some are heavily involved in student politics and others are less vocal. For many people, getting involved in the union can lead to a job, fun and a whole new group of friends. If an active union appeals to you find out more by logging on to the student union websites (see our list of addresses on page 112).

Which one of the following is you?

  1) *It's important to me to go to a university with a culturally diverse population.*

  2) *I'm not bothered whether my university is culturally diverse.*

  3) *What's cultural diversity?*

If you chose number one, then go to page 50 to find out which universities gave themselves an excellent rating for cultural diversity.

Which one of the following is you?

  1) *I want university to be a big family. I love bumping into friends as I walk around town.*

  2) *Get me to a sprawling metropolis – small places make me feel claustrophobic. I like to see people when I choose.*

  3) *I'm not really bothered – either way I'm happy.*

In a smaller university town such as St Andrews, the students are a large part of the town, and the likelihood is that you will bump into fellow students wherever you go. In larger cities, such as Manchester or London, you have the option to have a more anonymous student experience if you choose.

TOP TIP

'MY BIGGEST PIECE OF ADVICE FOR
PROSPECTIVE STUDENTS WOULD BE TO
RELAX IN YOUR FIRST YEAR. DON'T GET TOO
STRESSED ABOUT MAKING FRIENDS – JUST
TRY AND HAVE FUN. EVERYTHING USUALLY
WORKS OUT FINE – UNIVERSITY OFFERS A
GREAT EXPERIENCE AND LOTS OF FUN.'

Recent graduate.

What the unions said

Imagine you could contact over 60 student unions across the country and ask
for some insider information about what life at their university is really like. Well,
you don't have to imagine it – we've done it for you!

We've scoured the UK from Bournemouth to Belfast and talked to a selection of
student unions to find out about student life in universities across Britain. We
asked them to rate their university from excellent to poor on a range of issues.
Read on to find out how an official representative of the union rated lifestyle at
their university.

University	Food in halls	Accommodation in halls	Ample student accommodation	Union activity	Gym/sports facilities	Cultural diversity	Environmentally conscious policy	Equal opps policy	Disabled access	Attractive campus	Transport links
University of Abertay Dundee	very poor	good	excellent	good	good	excellent	fair	excellent	good	fair	excellent
University of Wales, Aberystwyth	quite poor	fair	excellent	excellent	good	excellent	excellent	excellent	good	excellent	good
Aston University	n/a	good***** *(both excellent and fair offered)*	excellent	excellent	fair	excellent	good	excellent	excellent	excellent	excellent
University of Wales, Bangor	good	excellent	good	excellent	excellent	excellent	fair	excellent	good	excellent	good
University of Bath	n/a	fair	good	good	excellent	excellent	fair	good	good	quite poor	good
Bath Spa University College	n/a	good	fair	excellent	fair	good	good	excellent	fair	excellent	good
University of Birmingham	fair	good*****	good	excellent	excellent	fair	excellent	good	fair	excellent	excellent
Bournemouth University	n/a	good	fair	excellent	very poor	quite poor	good	excellent	excellent	fair	fair
University of Bradford	n/a	good	good	excellent	good	excellent	good	excellent	fair	fair	good
University of Bristol	good	excellent	good	excellent	good	good	excellent	fair	fair	good	good
Buckinghamshire Chilterns University College	n/a	good/fair	fair	good	good/fair*	excellent	good	good	fair	good/fair	good/fair*
University of Cambridge	fair	good	excellent	good	excellent	good	good	good	good	excellent	good
Cardiff University	good	good	good	excellent	good	excellent	fair	good	fair	excellent	excellent
University of Central England (UCE)	fair	good	excellent	excellent	good	excellent	fair	good	good	fair	good
University of Central Lancashire (UCLAN)	n/a	good	excellent	excellent	excellent	excellent	good	excellent	excellent	excellent	excellent
De Montfort University	n/a	good	excellent	excellent	fair	excellent	excellent	excellent	fair	excellent	good
University of Derby	n/a	good	good	excellent	fair	good	good	good	good	excellent	excellent

University	Transport links	Attractive campus	Disabled access	Equal opps policy	Environmentally conscious policy	Cultural diversity	Gym/sports facilities	Union activity	Ample student accommodation	Accommodation in halls	Food in halls
University of Durham	excellent	excellent	fair	excellent	good	fair	good	excellent	good	excellent	good
University of East Anglia (UEA)	good	good	fair	excellent	excellent	fair	excellent	excellent	quite poor	good	quite poor
University of East London	excellent	good	excellent	excellent	fair	excellent	fair	good	fair	fair	n/a
Edge Hill College	fair	excellent	excellent	excellent	excellent	good	excellent	excellent	excellent	fair	good
University of Edinburgh	excellent	excellent	excellent	excellent	good	good	excellent	excellent	excellent	good	excellent
University of Essex	good	fair	good	excellent	excellent	excellent	excellent	excellent	fair	excellent	n/a
University of Exeter	good	excellent	good	good	good	quite poor	excellent	excellent	excellent	good	fair
University of Glamorgan	good	good	fair	excellent	excellent	excellent	excellent	good	good	good	n/a
University of Glasgow	good	excellent	good	good	fair	fair	excellent	excellent	quite poor	good	fair
Glasgow Caledonian University	excellent	excellent	good	excellent	fair		good	good	fair	good	n/a
University of Gloucestershire	good	excellent	good	excellent	good	excellent	excellent	excellent	excellent	excellent	n/a
Heriot-Watt University	good	excellent	good	excellent	good	excellent	excellent	excellent	good	good	fair
University of Huddersfield	good	good	good	good	fair	good	excellent	excellent	good	fair	n/a
University of Hull	excellent	excellent	good	good	fair	excellent	excellent	excellent	excellent	fair	fair
Imperial College London	excellent	excellent	good	good	excellent	excellent	fair	excellent	good	good	quite poor
Keele University	excellent	excellent	excellent	excellent	good	good	good	excellent	good	fair	good
University of Kent	quite poor	excellent	quite poor	good	fair	good	good	good	quite poor	fair	fair
King's College London	excellent	fair	quite poor	excellent	good	excellent	quite poor	excellent	good		quite poor
Lancaster University	excellent	good	good	good	good	fair	fair	excellent	excellent	good	
University of Leeds	excellent	excellent	excellent	excellent	excellent	excellent	fair	excellent	excellent	excellent	good

University	Food in halls	Accommodation in halls	Ample student accommodation	Union activity	Gym/sports facilities	Cultural diversity	Environmentally conscious policy	Equal opps policy	Disabled access	Attractive campus	Transport links
University of Lincoln	n/a	excellent	quite poor	fair	fair	fair	good	good	good	good	quite poor
University of Liverpool	fair	fair	good	excellent	fair	fair	good	good	quite poor	fair	good
Liverpool Hope University College	good	good	good	good	fair	excellent	good	good	good	excellent	fair
Liverpool John Moores University	n/a	good	excellent	excellent	good	excellent	good	good	good	good	good
London Metropolitan University	fair	good	good	excellent	good	excellent	good	excellent	fair	fair	excellent
London School of Economics and Political Science (LSE)	fair	good	good	excellent	good	excellent	good	excellent	quite poor	quite poor	excellent
Loughborough University	good	good	excellent	excellent	excellent	fair	good	good	good	excellent	fair
Manchester Metropolitan University	n/a	good	good	excellent	good	excellent	good	excellent	good	good	excellent
University of Newcastle Upon Tyne	fair	good	excellent	excellent	excellent	excellent	good	excellent	good	excellent	excellent
University College Northampton (UCN)	n/a	good	good	good	quite poor	good	good	good	fair	good**	good
University of Oxford	good	good	good	excellent	excellent	fair	good	fair	fair	excellent	excellent
Oxford Brookes University	fair	good	fair	excellent	excellent	excellent	good	good	good	good	good
University of Paisley	n/a	good	good	excellent	good	excellent	fair	excellent	good	good	excellent
University of Plymouth	fair	good	excellent	excellent	fair	good	very poor	good	good	excellent	excellent
University of Portsmouth	good	good	good	excellent	excellent	good	fair	excellent	good	excellent	excellent
Queen's University, Belfast	good	excellent	good	excellent	good	fair	good	good	good	excellent	excellent

University	Food in halls	Accommodation in halls	Ample student accommodation	Union activity	Gym/sports facilities	Cultural diversity	Environmentally conscious policy	Equal opps policy	Disabled access	Attractive campus	Transport links
University of Reading	quite poor	good	good	excellent	good	good	good	excellent	excellent	excellent	excellent
Royal Holloway, University of London	fair	excellent	good	excellent	fair	excellent	good	good	good	excellent	good
University of St Andrews	good	excellent	good	excellent	good	fair	excellent	excellent	fair	excellent	fair
University of Sheffield	good	excellent	excellent	excellent	excellent	excellent	excellent	excellent	excellent	excellent	excellent
Sheffield Hallam University	good	good	excellent	good	excellent	excellent	fair	excellent	fair	excellent	excellent
University of Southampton	fair	good	good	good	excellent	good	quite poor	excellent	good	excellent	good
Southampton Institute	n/a	good	good	good	quite poor	fair	fair	good	good	fair	excellent
University of Sunderland	n/a	good	excellent	excellent	fair	good	excellent	excellent	good	good	good
University of Surrey	n/a	good	fair	excellent	fair	excellent	fair	excellent	quite poor	excellent	excellent
University of Sussex	n/a	good	good	fair	good	excellent	good	excellent	fair***	excellent	good
University of Wales, Swansea	quite poor	good	fair	excellent	excellent	excellent	good	excellent	good	good	good
University of Warwick	n/a	good	fair	excellent	excellent	excellent	good	fair	good	excellent	good
University of Wolverhampton	n/a	good	good	good	excellent	excellent	fair	excellent	good	good	good
University of York	good	good	excellent/poor****	excellent	fair	very poor	fair	good	good	good	excellent

*Varies across campuses
**Two campuses: Park is excellent while Avenue is fair
*** In the process of being upgraded to good
**** For first-year students with relevant disabilities and international students, accommodation is guaranteed, so excellent for those groups, for others quite poor.
***** Mostly excellent except for one or two older halls

I WISH I'D KNOWN . . .

'I wish I'd looked at halls before I'd moved here. I'd have picked a different hall.'
– Student from Cardiff.

I WISH I'D KNOWN . . .

'I wish I'd known how far you have to travel between campuses.' – Student
from University of Central England (UCE).

Universities in the UK vary enormously in the facilities they provide and the
lifestyle they offer; these are a selection of the self-confessed best and worst:

Excellent and good food in halls

Cardiff University; University of Durham; University of Edinburgh; Keele
University; University of Leeds; Liverpool Hope University College;
Loughborough University; University of Oxford; University of Portsmouth;
Queen's University, Belfast; University of St Andrews; University of Sheffield;
Sheffield Hallam University; University of York.

Very poor and quite poor food in halls

University of Abertay Dundee; University of Wales, Aberystwyth; University of
East Anglia (UEA); Imperial College of Science, Technology and Medicine;
Lancaster University; University of Wales, Swansea.

Excellent accommodation in halls

University of Wales, Bangor; University of Birmingham; University of Bristol;
University of Durham; University of Gloucestershire; University of Leeds;
University of Lincoln; Queen's University, Belfast; Royal Holloway, London;
University of St Andrews; University of Sheffield.

Fair accommodation in halls

University of Wales, Aberystwyth; University of East London; Edge Hill College; University of Huddersfield; University of Hull; University of Kent.

SPOTLIGHT ON CAMPUS AND ACCOMMODATION

'At Sussex, the campus is very green – it's actually in a National Park. It's on the edge of town and so is a good mix of the urban and the rural. It was designed by Basil Spence – a sixties' architectural guru. His style is quite extreme – you could love it or hate it. But it is architecturally significant. Accommodation at Sussex is both fair and good. There is a wide variety of choice for student accommodation. East Slope is definitely grottier than Lewis. But East Slope has got the best social life – so in a way the grottier the better in terms of fun!' – Student from the University of Sussex.

'I spent one year in Queen's residential accommodation which is good and improving. I spent my next couple of years in the private sector where accommodation was OK but less good than in Queen's accommodation. The university is in the process of spending a lot of money on facilities across the board – there is currently a lot of money being put into gyms and sports facilities.' – Student from Queen's University, Belfast.

'I chose the University of East London (UEL) because of the course and because I wanted to be in London. I live in halls, at Docklands – the newest one. It's amazing. Docklands has been voted one of the best halls in England. Although I have to say some of the other UEL halls aren't so good. Docklands has even got things like heated towel rails! Around the Docklands campus there's not much going in terms of nightclubs and bars. If you want to go to a good nightclub in the centre of London it will cost you £20 to get back – so not many students can afford that very often. On the other hand you are in London, so you can go and see everything you want to in terms of culture and life.' – Student from the University of East London.

'There are two campuses. In terms of attractiveness, Park is excellent, while Avenue is fair.' – Student from University College Northampton.

'As well as good accommodation in halls, there's lots of private accommodation that still feels very student friendly.' – Student from Swansea University.

'The community feel of the campus is a major positive factor.' – Student from Keele University.

'I wish I'd known which halls were the fun ones before I came. As a general rule, Arthur Vicks is quiet while Rootes is party-central. Whitefields is also good as there are around 13 people per flat. In Warwick people live close to each other so there is a real community feel. But it's not in the centre of a bustling town – a minority of students complain about that. Accommodation in halls is good but expensive.' – Student from Warwick University.

'Get some information about the different colleges so you can you can make an informed choice about which one to pick.' – Student from Durham University.

Gym/sports facilities rated as excellent

University of Wales, Bangor; University of Bath; University of Birmingham; University of Cambridge; University of Central Lancashire (UCLAN); University of East Anglia (UEA); Edge Hill College; University of Edinburgh; University of Exeter; University of Glamorgan; University of Glasgow; University of Gloucestershire; Heriot-Watt University; University of Huddersfield; University of Hull; London School of Economics and Political Science (LSE); Loughborough University; University of Newcastle; Oxford Brookes University; University of Portsmouth; University of Sheffield; Sheffield Hallam University; University of Wales, Swansea; University of Warwick; University of Wolverhampton.

Gym/sports facilities rated as very poor and quite poor

Bournemouth University; King's College London; University College Northampton (UCN); Southampton Institute.

Cultural diversity rated as excellent

University of Abertay Dundee; University of Wales, Aberystwyth; Aston University; University of Wales, Bangor; University of Bath; University of Bradford; Cardiff University; University of Central England (UCE); University of Central Lancashire (UCLAN); De Montfort University; University of East London; University of Glamorgan; University of Gloucestershire; Heriot-Watt University; University of Hull; Imperial College; King's College London; University of Leeds; Liverpool Hope University College; Liverpool John Moores University; London Metropolitan; University; London School of Economics and Political Science (LSE); Manchester Metropolitan University; University of Newcastle Upon Tyne; Oxford Brookes University; Royal Holloway, University of London; University of Sheffield; Sheffield Hallam University; University of Surrey; University of Sussex; University of Wales, Swansea; University of Warwick; University of Wolverhampton.

Cultural diversity rated as quite poor and very poor

Bournemouth University; University of Exeter; University of York.

Environmentally conscious policy rated as excellent

University of Wales, Aberystwyth; University of Birmingham; University of Bristol; De Montfort University; University of East Anglia (UEA); Edge Hill College;

University of Glamorgan; Imperial College London; University of Leeds; University of St Andrews; University of Sheffield; University of Sunderland.

Environmentally conscious policy rated as very poor

University of Plymouth.

I WISH I'D KNOWN . . .

'... that everyone brings toasters, kettles, plates, cutlery and you suddenly have more toasters than Argos.' – Student from Sheffield Hallam.

I WISH I'D KNOWN . . .

'There are lots of hills – Sheffield's built on seven hills.' – Student from Sheffield University.

I WISH I'D KNOWN . . .

'... the distance of halls from the city centre and uni campus – kept me fit for a year though.' – Student from Sunderland University.

Equal opportunities policy rated as excellent

University of Abertay Dundee; University of Wales, Aberystwyth; Aston University; University of Wales, Bangor; Bath Spa University College; Bournemouth University; University of Bradford; University of Central Lancashire (UCLAN); De Montfort University; University of Durham; University of East Anglia (UEA); University of East London; Edge Hill College; University of Edinburgh; University of Glamorgan; Glasgow Caledonian University; University of Gloucestershire; Heriot-Watt University; Keele University; King's College, London; University of Leeds; London Metropolitan University; London School of Economics and Political Science (LSE); Manchester Metropolitan University; University of Newcastle Upon Tyne; University of Portsmouth; University of St

Andrews; University of Sheffield; Sheffield Hallam University; University of Sunderland; University of Surrey; University of Sussex; University of Wales, Swansea; University of Wolverhampton.

SPOTLIGHT ON UNION ACTIVITY

'I feel a bit mixed about UEL. On the one hand there is so much potential and we are all part of a developing community – anyone can set up any society they want. But because we're in London and everything is happening in this capital city, people don't focus so much on making fun for themselves – so I don't think there's a great sense of community. I think that happens more in universities in smaller places like St Andrews, for example, where the student union has to be a central focus of the student experience.' – Student from University of East London.

'There aren't the biggest amount of gigs in the world put on by the students' union – then again you're in London. It's not like there is a shortage in the city itself.' – Student from King's College London.

'The union here is quite left wing and politically active.' – Student from the University of Warwick.

'Sussex Union's activity in terms of entertainments isn't that strong – there's just no need: Brighton's got such amazing clubs and so much going on, the union can't compete.' – Student from the University of Sussex.

Disabled access rated as excellent

Aston University; Bournemouth University; University of Central Lancashire (UCLAN); University of East London; Edge Hill College; University of Edinburgh; Keele University; University of Leeds; Queen's University Belfast; University of Sheffield.

Disabled access rated as quite poor

University of Kent; King's College, London; London School of Economics and Political Science (LSE); University of Surrey.

'Disabled access at Sussex is currently being upgraded – for example, we've just installed a lift in the student union.' – Student from the University of Sussex.

Disabled students can find out more information from the *Disabled Students' Guide to University 2005*, edited by Emma Caprez and published by Trotman.

Attractive campus (rated as excellent)

University of Wales, Aberystwyth; Aston University; University of Wales, Bangor; Bath Spa University College; University of Birmingham; University of Cambridge; Cardiff University; University of Central Lancashire (UCLAN); De Montfort University; University of Derby; University of Durham; Edge Hill College; University of Edinburgh; University of Exeter; University of Glasgow; Glasgow Caledonian University; University of Gloucestershire; Heriot-Watt University; University of Hull; Imperial College London; Keele University; University of Kent; University of Leeds; Liverpool Hope University College; Loughborough University; University of Newcastle Upon Tyne; University of Plymouth; University of Portsmouth; Queen's University, Belfast; Royal Holloway, University of London; University of St Andrews; University of Sheffield; Sheffield Hallam University; University of Surrey; University of Sussex; University of Warwick.

Unattractive campuses

University of Bath; London School of Economics and Political Science (LSE).

Transport links rated excellent

University of Abertay Dundee; Aston University; University of Birmingham; University of Central Lancashire (UCLAN); University of Derby; University of Durham; University of East London; University of Edinburgh; Glasgow Caledonian University; University of Hull; Imperial College London; Keele University; King's College London; University of Lancaster; University of Leeds; London Metropolitan University; London School of Economics and Political Science (LSE); Manchester Metropolitan University; University of Newcastle Upon Tyne; University of Plymouth; University of Portsmouth; University of Sheffield; Sheffield Hallam University; Southampton Institute; University of York.

Transport links rated quite poor

University of Kent; University of Lincoln.

> 'Birmingham University's got its own train station called University and four different buses that go there – so transport is excellent.' – Student from Birmingham University.

I WISH I'D KNOWN . . .

'The train service to London is a nightmare. It takes 1 hour 45 minutes to get there. Hopefully this will change as the rail links are improved in future.' – Student from the University of Kent.

Other useful lifestyle rankings

Good facilities will have an impact on your student experience. The best way to find out about the facilities is to go and look at them. In the meantime read *The Times'* list of spending on university facilities given below.

Top ten for facilities spending

1. University of Wales Institute, Cardiff

2. Imperial College, London

3. University of Bath

4. University of Oxford

5. Royal Holloway, University of London

6. University of Surrey, Roehampton

7. University of Durham

8. University of Leicester

9. Loughborough University

10. University of East Anglia (UEA)

| **SOURCE:** *The Times Good University Guide 2005*/HESA |

Bottom ten for facilities spending (best to worst)

1. Napier University
2. Anglia Polytechnic University
3. University of Exeter
4. De Montfort University
5. University of Abertay Dundee
6. University of Gloucestershire
7. Glasgow Caledonian University
8. Bournemouth University
9. University of Middlesex
10. Thames Valley University

| SOURCE: *The Times Good University Guide 2005*/HESA |

The atmosphere in your university town will affect you. The best gay nightlife is likely to be found in a place with a thriving gay community. The *Guardian* recently drew up a gay map to show the places with the highest gay populations in England and Wales.

Gayest places in England and Wales

1. Brighton
2. London
3. Manchester
4. Blackpool, Lancashire
5. Bournemouth, Dorset
6. Cambridge
7. Nottingham
8. Bristol
9. Oxford
10. Lewes, East Sussex

The least gay places in England and Wales

1. Solihull, West Midlands

2. West Lindsey, Lincolnshire

3. Hartlepool, Cleveland

4. Easington, County Durham

5. Castle Morpeth, Northumberland

6. Wansbeck, Northumberland

7. Eden, Cumbria

8. Teesdale, County Durham

9. Redcar, Cleveland

10. Castle Point, Essex

| SOURCE: 'Location, Location, Orientation' by Julie Bindel – The *Guardian Weekend* 27 March 2004 |

'At Sussex, the Lesbian Gay and Bi Society is very active and has a strong presence. And many students are politically active.' – Student from Sussex University.

Safety is a big issue for students. Often on foot and likely to be living in rented accommodation in the less pleasant parts of town, it's a good idea to find out crime rates in the town you are moving to. Our table below, compiled by Endesleigh Insurance, shows university towns with the highest and lowest incidence of student claims made for break-ins. If you can, find out from students who are already studying at the university what the crime rate is like.

Top ten least safe university towns

1. Manchester

2. Leeds

3. Nottingham

4. Sheffield

5. Bristol

6. Birmingham

7. Liverpool

8. York

9. Glasgow

10. Newcastle Upon Tyne

Top ten safest university towns

1. Edinburgh

2. Swansea

3. Cambridge

4. Bath

5. Portsmouth

6. Brighton

7. Durham

8. Southampton

9. Stoke on Trent

10 Norwich

| **SOURCE:** Endesleigh Insurance – tables based on number of claims for break-ins |

'I feel safe at Aston as there's a low crime rate round here.' – Student from Aston University.

Male:female ratio – unis where the testosterone's pumping

- **Architectural Association**   3:2
- **Dentistry @ Barts and The London**   3:2
- **University of Bath**   4:3
- **Bolton Institute**   11:9
- **Bristol Old Vic**   3:2
- **University of Buckingham**   5:4
- **Camborne School of Mines**   4:1

- **Farnborough College** 3:2
- **Guildhall School of Music and Drama** 3:2
- **Harper Adams University College** 3:2
- **Heythrop College** 3:2
- **Leeds College of Music** 4:1
- **London Bible College** 3:2
- **London Business School** 3:1
- **London College of Printing** 3:2
- **London Film School** 4:1
- **Loughborough University** 5:3
- **Manchester Business School** 3:1
- **Oak Hill College** 5:1
- **University of Oxford** 3:2
- **Scottish Agricultural College** 3:2
- **Southampton Institute** 3:2
- **Spurgeon's College** 6:1
- **University of Manchester Institute of Science and Technology** 7:3

| **SOURCE:** Data from *Student Book 2004*, Klaus Boehm and Jenny Lees-Spalding, Trotman |

Female:male ratio – unis where women are in the majority

- **Birmingham Conservatoire** 5:3
- **Bradford College** 2:1
- **Central Saint Martin's** 2:1
- **Central School of Speech and Drama** 2:1
- **Chester College** 3:1
- **Chichester University College** 3:1
- **Colchester Institute** 5:2
- **Courtauld Institute** 3:1
- **University of East Anglia (UEA)** 3:1
- **Edge Hill College** 2:1
- **Glasgow School of Art** 2:1

- **King Alfred's College Winchester**   3:1
- **Laban College**   4:1
- **Leeds College of Music**   4:1
- **London College of Fashion**   5:1
- **Queen Margaret University College**   4:1
- **Roehampton (USR)**   3:1
- **Royal Veterinary College**   3:1
- **St Martin's College**   3:1
- **Trinity College Carmarthen**   4:1
- **Wimbledon School of Art**   7:3
- **Winchester School of Art**   3:1
- **York St John**   3:1

| **Source:** Tables compiled from data in the *Student Book 2004*, Klaus Boehm and Jenny Lees-Spalding, Trotman |

I WISH I'D KNOWN . . .

'I wish I'd known how hilly Bradford is and how it rains for the majority of the year!' – Student from Bradford.

I WISH I'D KNOWN . . .

'Nothing – I've had a fantastic time, although my mate says he wishes someone had told him Bristol was hilly.' – Student from Bristol.

Notice how many students complain about hills? That's because most students spend a lot of time walking – it's much cheaper than public transport!

And with all that walking there's one thing you can guarantee students know about – the weather. Read on to find out which university towns are the coldest and hottest.

Sizzling students – for those who want to warm it up

Top ten warmest cities (average temperature in centigrade)

1. London	11.7
2. {Cardiff	11.2
{Southampton	11.2
4. Bristol	11.1
5. Plymouth	11.0
6. Brighton	10.8
7. Reading	10.7
8. Bath	10.6
9. Exeter	10.6
10. Manchester	10.5

Chillin at college – for those who prefer cooler climes

Top ten coldest cities (average temperature in centigrade)

1. Aberdeen	8.1
2. {Glasgow	8.6
{Edinburgh	8.6
4. {Belfast	8.8
{Durham	8.8
6. St Andrews	8.9
7. Dundee	9.0
8. Leicester	9.1
9. Derby	9.4
10. Nottingham	9.5

| SOURCE: data compiled by Met Office |

I WISH I'D KNOWN . . .

'The weather in Bournemouth is phenomenal – we just have such great weather!' – Student from the University of Bournemouth.

I WISH I'D KNOWN . . .

'How much it rains in the winter!' – Student from Lancaster University.

The worst things about university

1. **Having little money**
2. **Being in debt**
3. **No regular income**
4. **Juggling university with other commitments**
5. **Needing to work and study at the same time**

| **SOURCE:** *UNITE Student Living Report 2004* |

I WISH I'D KNOWN . . .

'I wish I'd got involved in all the extra-curricular stuff sooner. I think Queen's is a fantastic place to study.' – Student from Queen's, Belfast.

I WISH I'D KNOWN . . .

'... how many hills there were in Bangor – not the best after a few too many.' – Student from Bangor.

I WISH I'D KNOWN . . .

'The cost of living' – Student from Bath.

CHAPTER FOUR

Ultimate Fun

Most students, no matter how skint or hard working, manage to fit in a lot of fun during their degree. University is a time to meet like-minded people and live in a community with people from different backgrounds from all over the UK. It's a time to expand your mind and social circle. So it is important to look into the social life available at your prospective university. Read our ultimate fun rankings and be inspired to think about what you want from your university social life.

Social scene

Which one of the following is you?

1) *I love urban nightlife. I'm into clubbing and want to be at the centre of it all.*

2) *Give me the rural life any day. I love walking in the countryside and going to pubs with friends.*

3) *I want a bit of both – some city life, but easy access to the countryside too.*

Think about what you enjoy. Is life in a big city such as London, Liverpool or Manchester for you, or would you prefer a quieter pace of life in a countryside setting?

Which one of the following is you?

1) *I'm a teetotaller: bars and pubs don't interest me.*

2) *I want to go somewhere with fantastic bars and pubs.*

3) *I'm not really bothered about bars and pubs.*

If bars and pubs are your thing, check out our student union ratings below.

Which one of the following is you?

1) *Music is my life – I've got to be able to see great live music.*

2) *What do you think CDs are for?*

3) *I'd rather be able to see the sea.*

If music is the most important thing in your life, check out our student union ratings below.

Which one of the following is you?

1) *Wouldn't you just die without Almodavar?*

2) *Almo who?*

3) *Arty-farty cinema just isn't my thing.*

If art-house films are your thing, check out our student ratings below.

If none of the above are you, think what it is that you really enjoy doing, hopefully you can find a university with a good course that can also cater to your social side.

What the unions said

We asked a selection of student unions to rate some of the fun stuff at their universities. Here's what they had to say:

University	Freshers' week	Local music venues	Local clubs	Local art-house cinemas	Local theatres (student and other)	Local pubs
University of Abertay Dundee	excellent	good	good	excellent	good	excellent
University of Wales, Aberystwyth	excellent	good	fair	excellent	excellent	excellent
Aston University	excellent	excellent	excellent	good	excellent	excellent
University of Wales, Bangor	excellent	excellent	good	good	excellent	excellent
University of Bath	excellent	good	fair	excellent	good	excellent
Bath Spa University College	excellent	excellent	good	fair	fair	excellent
University of Birmingham	good	excellent	excellent	excellent	excellent	excellent
Bournemouth University	excellent	fair	excellent	quite poor	quite poor	excellent
University of Bradford	good	fair	fair	excellent	excellent	excellent
University of Bristol	excellent	excellent	good	quite poor	good	fair
Buckinghamshire Chilterns University College	good	fair	fair	fair	good	good
Cambridge University	excellent	fair	very poor	excellent	excellent	excellent
Cardiff University	excellent	excellent	excellent	good	good	excellent
University of Central England (UCE)	excellent	fair	good	good	good	good
University of Central Lancashire (UCLAN)	excellent	fair	good		good	excellent
De Montfort University	excellent	excellent	excellent	good	good	excellent
University of Derby	excellent	good	good	good	fair	good
University of Durham	excellent	good	good	fair	good	good
University of East Anglia (UEA)	fair	good	good	excellent	excellent	excellent

University	Freshers' week	Local music venues	Local clubs	Local art-house cinemas	Local theatres (student and other)	Local pubs
University of East London	quite poor	quite poor	quite poor	quite poor	quite poor	quite poor
Edge Hill College	good	fair	good	fair	fair	good
University of Edinburgh	excellent	good	excellent	excellent	excellent	excellent
University of Essex	excellent	fair	fair	quite poor	fair	good
University of Exeter	excellent	good	fair	good	good	excellent
University of Glamorgan	excellent	quite poor	good	excellent	good	good
University of Glasgow	good	excellent	excellent	excellent	excellent	excellent
Glasgow Caledonian University	excellent	excellent	good	good	good	excellent
University of Gloucestershire	excellent	good	fair	good	good	good
Heriot-Watt University	excellent	excellent	fair	good	good	good
University of Huddersfield	good	fair	excellent	quite poor	good	excellent
University of Hull	excellent	good	excellent	fair	fair	excellent
Imperial College London	excellent	good	excellent	excellent	excellent	fair
Keele University	good	good	good	quite poor	good	good
University of Kent	excellent	good	good	excellent	good	good
King's College London	fair	excellent	excellent	excellent	excellent	excellent
Lancaster University	excellent	fair	excellent	fair	fair	good
University of Leeds	excellent	excellent	excellent	excellent	excellent	excellent
University of Lincoln	fair	quite poor	fair	very poor	fair	fair
University of Liverpool	excellent	good	excellent	excellent	excellent	good
Liverpool Hope University College	excellent	good	good	fair	excellent	good

University	Freshers' week	Local music venues	Local clubs	Local art-house cinemas	Local theatres (student and other)	Local pubs
Liverpool John Moores University	excellent	excellent	excellent	excellent	excellent	good
London Metropolitan University	good	excellent	excellent	good	excellent	excellent
London School of Economics and Political Science (LSE)	excellent	excellent	excellent	excellent	excellent	excellent
Loughborough University	excellent	fair	fair	quite poor	fair	good
Manchester Metropolitan University	excellent	excellent	excellent	excellent	excellent	excellent
University of Newcastle Upon Tyne	excellent	good	excellent	excellent	excellent	excellent
University College Northampton (UCN)	excellent	good	good	fair	fair	excellent
University of Oxford	fair	excellent	good	excellent	excellent	excellent
Oxford Brookes University	excellent	good	fair	excellent	excellent	good
University of Paisley	excellent	good	good	quite poor	quite poor	excellent
University of Plymouth	excellent	fair	fair	fair	fair	good
University of Portsmouth	excellent	excellent	excellent	fair	quite poor	excellent
Queen's University, Belfast	excellent	excellent	excellent	excellent	excellent	excellent
Reading University	banging (excellent)	good	fair	fair	good	good
Royal Holloway, University of London	excellent	fair	quite poor	good	?	excellent
University of St Andrews	excellent	fair	quite poor	quite poor	fair	excellent
University of Sheffield	excellent	excellent	excellent	excellent	excellent	excellent
Sheffield Hallam University	good	good	fair	excellent	excellent	good
University of Southampton	good	fair	good	quite poor	fair	excellent

University	Freshers' week	Local music venues	Local clubs	Local art-house cinemas	Local theatres (student and other)	Local pubs
Southampton Institute	good	fair	good	fair	good	excellent
University of Sunderland	excellent	fair	good	quite poor	good	excellent
University of Surrey	excellent	quite poor	quite poor	fair	fair	good
University of Sussex	good	excellent	excellent	excellent	excellent	excellent
University of Wales, Swansea	good	fair	good	good	good	excellent
Warwick University	excellent	fair	fair	good	good	excellent
University of Wolverhampton	good	excellent	fair	excellent	excellent	excellent
University of York	excellent	fair	fair	excellent	good	excellent

Which universities have the most fun? These are a selection of the self-confessed best and worst:

Local music venues excellent

Aston University; University of Wales, Bangor; Bath Spa University College; University of Birmingham; Cardiff University; De Montfort University; Glasgow Caledonian University; Heriot-Watt University; King's College, London; University of Leeds; Liverpool John Moores University; London Metropolitan University; London School of Economics and Political Science (LSE); University of Portsmouth; Queen's University, Belfast; University of Sheffield; University of Sussex; University of Wolverhampton.

Local music venues quite poor

University of East London; University of Glamorgan; University of Lincoln; University of Surrey.

Local clubs excellent

Aston University; University of Birmingham; Bournemouth University; Cardiff University; De Montfort University; University of Edinburgh; University of Glasgow; University of Hull; Imperial College London; King's College London; Lancaster University; University of Leeds; University of Liverpool; Liverpool John Moores University; London School of Economics and Political Science (LSE); London Metropolitan University; University of Newcastle Upon Tyne; University of Portsmouth; Queen's University, Belfast; University of Sheffield; University of Sussex.

Local clubs quite poor and very poor

University of East London; Royal Holloway, University of London; University of St Andrews; University of Surrey

Local art house cinemas excellent

University of Abertay Dundee; University of Wales, Aberystwyth; University of Bath; Queen's University, Belfast; University of Birmingham; University of Bradford; University of Cambridge; University of East Anglia; University of Edinburgh; University of Glamorgan; University of Glasgow; Imperial College London; University of Kent; King's College London; University of Leeds;

University of Liverpool; Liverpool John Moores University; University of Newcastle Upon Tyne; Oxford Brookes University; Queen's University, Belfast; University of Sheffield; Sheffield Hallam University; University of Sussex; University of Wolverhampton; University of York.

Local art house cinemas quite poor

University of East London; University of Huddersfield; Keele University; University of Lincoln (very poor); Loughborough University; University of St Andrews; University of Sunderland.

Local theatres student and other excellent

University of Wales, Aberystwyth; Aston University; University of Wales, Bangor; University of Birmingham; University of Bradford; University of Cambridge; University of East Anglia (UEA); University of Edinburgh; University of Glasgow; Imperial College London; King's College London; University of Leeds; University of Liverpool; Liverpool Hope University; Liverpool John Moores University; London Metropolitan University; London School of Economics and Political Science (LSE); University of Newcastle Upon Tyne; Oxford Brookes University; Queen's University Belfast; University of Sheffield; Sheffield Hallam University; University of Wolverhampton.

Local theatres student and other quite poor

University of East London; University of Portsmouth.

Other fun rankings

'Bournemouth University has got the best student nightclub in the country – The Old Firestation. It's got its own firepole and has a capacity of 1,200.' – Student from Bournemouth University.

We're not suggesting that the price of booze should be a factor in your decision-making process – but it's always best to be given all the facts …

Boozability – average beer prices in the UK

- **UK average**   £2.11
- **London**   £2.31
- **South East**   £2.26
- **East Anglia**   £2.24
- **South West**   £2.15
- **West Midlands**   £2.04
- **North**   £2.04
- **East Midlands**   £2.02
- **Scotland**   £2.02
- **Wales**   £2.01
- **Yorkshire**   £1.98
- **North West**   £1.90

| **Source:** Campaign for Real Ale 2002 |

I WISH I'D KNOWN . . .

'How the cheap price of beer in the city would seriously affect my grades!' –
Student from Portsmouth.

The University of Manchester is 'number one' for drugs and sex according
to a survey from the Adam Smith Institute 2000. This finding hit the
headlines in 2000.

I WISH I'D KNOWN . . .

'... that I was going to find it so difficult to leave ...!' – Student from
Edinburgh.

CHAPTER FIVE
Ultimate Jobs and Money

Part of the student experience is being strapped for cash while dreaming of a glittering future to come. Unfortunately, most students today leave university with a large debt – on average £12,000. Don't let this put you off going to university. As long as you've chosen well, a degree from a good university should pay out in higher earnings over your lifetime. Starting salaries for graduates in 2004 ranged from £15,000 to £35,000 a year according to *Students' Money Matters 2004* – that's a 3.9% increase on last year.

As many as 90% of students now work at some point during their degree according to Mandy Telford, President of the National Union of Students. The second most common reason for dropping out of university is financial difficulty according to the *UNITE Student Living Report 2004*. With money so tight, keeping an eye on your finances and budgeting are essential to reduce debt.

Jobs after university

A degree can increase your earning power in your lifetime. In their twenties, graduates can expect to earn around £6,000 more than non-graduates in the same age group. The difference is even greater by the time you reach your forties, when graduates earn around 76% more than non-graduates according to the Labour Force Survey 2003.

The work of graduates contributes about three times the cost of their salary to companies which cherry-pick the most academic students straight from university. This is the finding of the Association of Graduate Recruiters who say that graduate recruitment schemes add around £1 billion of 'added value' to the organisations with graduate recruitment schemes.

Many large organisations offer graduate recruitment schemes, from publishing to retail. Look into these as early as you can, as competition is fierce. If you do manage to get on one of these schemes you will benefit from loads of money being spent on your training and relative job security.

If you've done your research well into the reputation of your course and your university, and you've worked hard, with some determination you will find a job. Taking part in extra-curricular activities related to your future career will also help.

For more information on how a range of graduate recruiters rate universities in terms of employability read *From Learning to Earning* by Cliff Pettifor, published by Trotman.

Bottom ten courses for graduate employment and further study (worst to best)

1. **Art and Design**

2. **Italian**

3. **Drama, Dance and Cinematics**

4. **Communication and Media Studies**

5. **Iberian Languages**

6. **American Studies**

7. **Anthropology**

8. **Sociology**

9. **Russian**

10. **Psychology**

Source: *The Times Good University Guide 2005*/HESA – graduate employment refers to jobs which normally recruit graduates. This table is ranked by the sum of the 'positive' destinations – graduate employment and further study.

Top ten courses for graduate employment and further study

1. **Dentistry**

2. **Medicine**

3. **Nursing**

4. **Veterinary Medicine**

5. **Pharmacology and Pharmacy**

6. **Architecture**

7. **Civil Engineering**

8. **Other subjects allied to Medicine**

9. Education

10. Building

| **SOURCE:** *The Times Good University Guide 2005*/HESA – graduate employment refers to jobs that normally recruit graduates. |

Law graduates will earn the most in their lifetime – male lawyers will rake in an average salary of £35,000 a year compared to £26,100 a year for agricultural graduates and £27,400 for communication graduates.

(Source: *The Times* 28 April 2004, quoting research done at Warwick University by Ian Walker)

Over 95% of graduates employed or in further study after six months

Aberdeen University; University of Bristol; University of Cambridge; Canterbury Christ Church College; University of Wales Institute, Cardiff; Chichester University College; City University; University of Dundee; Glamorgan University; University of Gloucestershire; University of Hull; University of Kent; University of Leeds; University of Liverpool; Liverpool Hope University College; Loughborough University; Northern School of Contemporary Dance; Northumbria University; Nottingham Trent University; Oxford Brookes University; Queen Margaret University College; Queen's University Belfast; Robert Gordon University; Royal Academy of Music; Royal College of Music; Royal Northern College of Music; Royal Scottish Academy of Music and Drama; Royal Veterinary College; St George's Hospital Medical School; St Martin's College; St Mary's College; Salford University; School of Pharmacy; Sheffield University; University of Surrey; Swansea Institute; Trinity College of Music; Wimbledon School of Art; Worcester University College; Writtle College.

Under 90% of graduates employed or in further study after six months

University of Abertay Dundee; Bolton Institute; Dartington College of Arts; University of East London; Goldsmiths College; University of Greenwich; Kent Institute; University of Wales, Lampeter; University of Lincoln; London Institute; London Metropolitan University; Middlesex University; University of Paisley; Queen Mary, University of London; Ravensbourne College; Rose Bruford College;

Royal Agricultural College; Royal Holloway, University of London; School of Oriental and African Studies; University College London; Westminster University; Wolverhampton University.

| **SOURCE:** *Student Book 2005*, Klaus Boehm and Jenny Lees-Spalding, Trotman |

Money at university

SPOTLIGHT ON FINANCE

'I wish I'd known how to manage my finances better.' – Recent graduate from the University of Bournemouth.

'It's important to source out what further financial support is available. There are all kinds of schemes in place to support students financially and if I had known and taken advantage of them, I would have less student debt. I'm sure that this would arise across the survey.' – Recent graduate from the University of Derby.

'I left Warwick with around the same amount of student debt as everyone else: £10,000. But I don't really notice it – I pay it off at £40 a month.' – Recent graduate from the University of Warwick.

Read *Students' Money Matters 2004* by Gwenda Thomas for useful information on everything to do with student finance.

NEWS FLASH – NO TOP-UP FEES FOR GAP YEARERS IN 2005

Due to a late amendment to the HE Bill, students 'who apply during 2004/2005 for a place at university or college but who wish to defer entry until 2006, to take a Year Out, will not have to pay top-up fees of £3,000 a year for the duration of their courses.' (Source: www.ucas.com)

Most popular types of student work

- **Retail**
- **Bar work**
- **Catering**
- **Clerical/office**
- **Nursing/health care**
- **Call centre**
- **Teaching**
- **Work for the university**

| **SOURCE:** *UNITE Student Living Report 2004* |

I WISH I'D KNOWN . . .

'How expensive living in London is!' – Student from Imperial College London.

Top ways to save for university

1. **Full-time holiday job**
2. **Part-time holiday job**
3. **Part-time job during school term**
4. **Long-term savings**
5. **Saved money given as presents**

| **SOURCE:** *UNITE Student Living Report 2004* |

I WISH I'D KNOWN . . .

'There's nothing I wish I'd known before I came here. I've loved my time at UCN.' Student from University College Northampton.

Average weekly student living expenses

1. London	£242
2. Outer London	£208
3. South England	£173
4. Oxbridge	£148
5. Scotland	£141
6. Wales and West England	£129
7. Midlands	£128
8. North	£120

(Above figures include rent, food, socialising and entertainment, laundry, toiletries, telephone, travel, books, photocopying, clothes, travel home and utilities.)

| **SOURCE:** *Students' Money Matters 2004*, Gwenda Thomas, Trotman Publishing |

Average student rent

1. London	£150
2. South England	£82
3. Oxbridge	£77
4. Outer London	£68
5. Wales and West England	£56
6. Scotland	£57
7. Midlands	£54
8. North	£48

| **Source:** *Students' Money Matters 2004*, Gwenda Thomas, Trotman Publishing |

Most first-year students choose to stay in halls, as they are great places to meet other students. The price of university-managed accommodation varies according to the university and the type of accommodation package you opt for. Check out the table below to find out more:

Institution name	Cost of accommodation including meals £	Cost of accommodation with no food £	Cost of accommodation en suite, no food £
The University of Aberdeen	81.75 – 96.50		
University of Abertay Dundee		50.00	60.00
The University of Wales, Aberystwyth	65.20 – 79.16	35.62 – 60.77	63.76
The College of Agriculture, Food and Rural Enterprise	61.00	28.00	31.00
American InterContinental University – London		200.00	
Anglia Polytechnic University		48.13 – 91.00	65.50 – 76.59
Askham Bryan College	63.00 – 73.00	44.00	
Aston University		54.90 – 85.80	85.80
University of Wales, Bangor	77.00 – 89.00	47.00 – 54.00	65.00 – 68.00
Barony College	82.00	55.00	82.00
University of Bath		49.50 – 67.00	67.00 – 76.00
Bath Spa University College		57.00 – 73.25	83.75
Bell College		55.00	
The University of Birmingham	91.90 – 130.40	58.00 – 85.80	77.70 – 85.80
Birmingham College of Food, Tourism & Creative Studies (college accredited by Univ of Birmingham)		65.00	70.00
Bishop Burton College		40.00 – 50.00	55.00 – 60.00
Bishop Grosseteste College	76.50		
Bolton Institute of Higher Education		50.00	
Bournemouth University		58.00 – 74.00	66.00 – 74.00
The Arts Institute at Bournemouth			69.50

Institution name	Cost of accommodation including meals £	Cost of accommodation with no food £	Cost of accommodation en suite, no food £
The University of Bradford		46.20 – 53.10	71.50 – 72.31
Bradford College (an associate college of the University of Bradford)		51.50 – 75.00	75.00
University of Brighton		53.00 – 70.00	72.00 – 75.00
Brighton and Sussex Medical School		53.00 – 70.00	70.00 – 76.00
University of Bristol	83.00 – 110.00	39.00 – 79.00	
University of the West of England, Bristol		45.00 – 65.00	60.00 – 75.00
Brunel University		57.96	70.98
British School of Osteopathy		75.00 – 95.00	
Broxtowe College, Nottingham		73.00	73.00
The University of Buckingham		65.00 – 108.00	78.00
University of Cambridge	80.00 – 111.00	40.00 – 60.00	60.00 – 80.00
Canterbury Christ Church University College	80.00 – 85.00	68.00 – 73.00	
Capel Manor College, Enfield, Middlesex		75.00 – 85.00	
Cardiff University	58.00 – 67.00	41.00 – 53.00	50.00 – 56.00
University of Wales Institute, Cardiff	78.00 – 81.00	55.00 – 72.00	62.00 – 75.00
Carmarthenshire College		40.00 – 50.00	40.00 – 50.00
University of Central England in Birmingham	64.00 – 65.00	46.00 – 75.00	71.50 – 72.50
CECOS London College of IT and Management		45.00 – 60.00	
University of Central Lancashire		59.00	66.00
University College Chester	50.00 – 94.00	33.00 – 60.00	

Institution name	Cost of accommodation including meals £	Cost of accommodation with no food £	Cost of accommodation en suite, no food £
Chichester College	130.00 – 135.00	60.00 – 85.00	75.00 – 80.00
University College Chichester	95.00 – 110.00		
City University		89.04	89.04
City of Bristol College		68.00	
Cliff College	98.00		
Courtauld Institute of Art (University of London)	78.00 – 104.00	52.00 – 99.00	
Coventry University	76.00	37.00 – 64.00	57.00 – 64.00
Cumbria Institute of the Arts		50.00 – 52.00	52.00 – 55.00
Dartington College of Arts		53.50 – 59.00	
De Montfort University		45.00 – 65.00	66.00 – 75.00
University of Derby		41.00 – 60.00	71.00
Doncaster College		47.00	52.00
University of Dundee		55.00 – 58.00	86.00 – 94.00
The University of Durham	118.00 – 121.00	72.00	
University of East Anglia		46.34	60.97 – 72.24
East Lancashire Institute of Higher Education		48.00	
University of East London		49.50 – 75.00	
Edge Hill College of Higher Education (a higher education institution accredited by Lancaster Univ)	74.00	42.00 – 59.00	59.00
The University of Edinburgh	104.00 – 120.00	64.00 – 72.00	
The University of Essex		42.00 – 51.00	70.00 – 75.00

Institution name	Cost of accommodation including meals £	Cost of accommodation with no food £	Cost of accommodation en suite, no food £
European Business School, London	180.00 – 250.00		
University of Exeter	85.00 – 106.00	42.00 – 85.00	63.00 – 90.00
Falmouth College of Arts			72.00 – 79.00
University of Glamorgan		48.00 – 50.00	57.00 – 59.00
University of Glasgow	81.00 – 83.00	59.00	72.00 – 74.00
Glasgow Caledonian University		67.00	77.00
The Glasgow School of Art		56.00	64.00
The University of Gloucestershire		70.00	80.00
Goldsmiths College (University of London)		69.50 – 71.00	82.00 – 90.00
University of Greenwich		68.50 – 120.00	68.50 – 120.00
Grimsby College		55.00	
Harper Adams University College	73.00 – 99.75		
Herefordshire College of Technology		50.00	
Heriot-Watt University, Edinburgh	75.00 – 81.00	43.00 – 52.00	62.00
University of Hertfordshire		50.00 – 73.00	80.00 – 83.00
Highbury College			85.00
Holborn College	90.00 – 130.00	80.00 – 90.00	
The University of Hull	72.10 – 95.60	53.13 – 73.08	73.08
Hull York Medical School		55.00 – 62.00	
Imperial College London (University of London)	85.58 – 107.98	55.86 – 101.36	77.07 – 119.84
Keele University		51.00 – 58.00	83.00

Institution name	Cost of accommodation including meals £	Cost of accommodation with no food £	Cost of accommodation en suite, no food £
The University of Kent	68.60 – 81.27	56.98 – 65.31	77.91 – 90.72
Kent Institute of Art and Design		51.00 – 66.00	70.50 – 72.50
King Alfred's Winchester		67.00	74.00 – 79.00
King's College London (University of London)	94.00	52.00 – 91.00	91.00
Kingston University		55.50 – 75.50	
The University of Wales, Lampeter		41.00	50.00
Lancaster University		42.70 – 52.50	68.25 – 70.70
University of Leeds	60.00 – 110.00	40.00 – 67.00	57.00 – 67.00
Leeds Trinity & All Saints (accredited college of the University of Leeds)	74.63	61.58	86.06
Leeds Metropolitan University		48.00 – 68.00	72.00
University of Leicester	74.62 – 100.31	51.45 – 58.73	66.85 – 80.00
University of Lincoln			66.00 – 70.00
The University of Liverpool	81.30 – 93.87	57.47 – 61.59	64.19
Lincoln College		52.50	
Liverpool Hope University College	83.00	65.83	75.83
Liverpool John Moores University		49.00 – 89.00	67.00 – 89.00
The London Institute	111.50	58.00 – 114.00	
London Metropolitan University	89.00 – 92.00	79.00 – 82.00	
London School of Economics and Political Science (University of London)	72.00 – 112.00	53.00 – 103.00	96.00 – 112.00
London South Bank University		70.00 – 90.00	

Institution name	Cost of accommodation including meals £	Cost of accommodation with no food £	Cost of accommodation en suite, no food £
Loughborough College		55.00 – 65.00	55.00 – 65.00
Loughborough University	80.00 – 115.00	50.00 – 70.00	52.00 – 66.00
University of Luton		45.00 – 66.00	70.00 – 75.00
The University of Manchester	78.00 – 102.00	45.00 – 57.00	72.00 – 76.00
The Manchester Metropolitan University	77.00	47.50 – 81.00	76.00 – 81.00
Marjon – The College of St Mark & St John	66.00 – 75.00	55.00 – 70.00	
Medway School of Pharmacy		68.50 – 120.00	68.50 – 120.00
Middlesex University		63.00 – 69.00	70.00 – 75.00
Myerscough College	69.00 – 101.00		
Napier University, Edinburgh		62.00 – 65.00	
University of Newcastle Upon Tyne	68.60 – 93.80	43.47 – 58.38	60.97 – 70.21
Newman College of Higher Education	70.00 – 73.00	65.00	
University of Wales, Newport		46.75	56.00
University College Northampton		32.50 – 59.15	44.05 – 63.50
The Norwich School of Art and Design		45.00 – 65.00	
The North East Wales Institute of Higher Education			60.00 – 70.00
Northumbria University	81.00	53.50 – 63.50	75.00
Northumberland College		30.00	
Norwich City College of Further and Higher Education (a regional college of Anglia Polytechnic Univ)		44.00	
The University of Nottingham	77.00 – 115.00	48.00 – 68.00	68.00

Institution name	Cost of accommodation including meals £	Cost of accommodation with no food £	Cost of accommodation en suite, no food £
The Nottingham Trent University		58.00 – 69.49	72.15 – 76.17
Oxford University	126.24	83.28	
Oxford Brookes University	80.00	69.00 – 80.00	73.00 – 80.00
University of Paisley		45.00	
Pembrokeshire College (accredited college of University of Glamorgan)		45.00 – 65.00	
Peninsula Medical School		55.00 – 80.00	55.00 – 80.00
University of Plymouth		55.50 – 63.00	73.50 – 100.00
University of Portsmouth	83.00 – 98.00	60.00 – 92.00	75.00 – 97.00
Queen Margaret University College, Edinburgh	85.00	57.50	
Queen Mary, University of London	79.00 – 103.00	58.00 – 98.00	95.00 – 98.00
Queen's University Belfast	66.00	47.00 – 55.00	65.00
Ravensbourne College of Design and Communication		64.00	64.00
Reading College and School of Arts & Design		65.00	
The University of Reading	91.00 – 121.00	50.44 – 60.43	80.15
Regents Business School London	180 .00 – 275.00	180.00 – 275.00	180.00 – 275.00
Richmond, The American International University in London	175.00 – 200.00		
The Robert Gordon University		49.00 – 62.00	66.00 – 72.00
Royal Agricultural College	90.00 – 160.00		
Royal Holloway, University of London		56.00 – 84.00	84.00
Royal Veterinary College (University of London)	90.00 – 110.00		82.00

Institution name	Cost of accommodation including meals £	Cost of accommodation with no food £	Cost of accommodation en suite, no food £
Ruskin College Oxford	80.00 – 85.00		
Scottish Agricultural College	70.00 – 85.00	48.00 – 70.00	
The University of Salford	88.90	43.61	
Salisbury College	75.00 – 120.00		
Sandwell College		65.00	
School of Oriental and African Studies (University of London)	100.00 – 125.00		90.00 – 97.00
The School of Pharmacy (University of London)	90.00 – 100.00		
The University of Sheffield	83.79 – 92.15	62.65 – 66.99	76.65
Sheffield Hallam University	77.50	57.50	60.00 – 70.00
Sheffield College		60.00 – 80.00	60.00 – 80.00
St Martin's College, Lancaster; Ambleside; Carlisle; London (accredited college of Lancaster Univ)	82.50	58.00	85.00
Solihull College		60.00	
University of Southampton	86.87 – 116.69	48.30 – 78.21	78.21
Somerset College of Arts and Technology		56.00 – 60.00	
Southampton Institute		77.00 – 84.70	
South Devon College		45.00 – 65.00	65.00 – 85.00
Sparsholt College Hampshire	82.00 – 89.00		82.00
University of St Andrews	78.00 – 108.00	41.00 – 43.00	54.00 – 75.00
St George's Hospital Medical School (University of London)	95.88	58.60	
St Helens College (an associate college of Liverpool John Moores University)		52.00	

Institution name	Cost of accommodation including meals £	Cost of accommodation with no food £	Cost of accommodation en suite, no food £
St Mary's College	65.00 – 110.00	78.00	
Staffordshire University		44.00	64.00
The University of Stirling		54.00	65.00
The University of Strathclyde		43.60	63.80 – 68.75
Stranmillis University College: A College of Queen's University Belfast	68.00		
University of Sunderland		50.00	64.00 – 90.00
University of Surrey		45.00	82.00
The Surrey Institute of Art and Design, University College		47.00	62.00 – 64.00
University of Sussex		60.00	70.00 – 76.00
University of Wales Swansea	64.80 – 79.50	45.80	58.80 – 69.50
Swansea Institute of Higher Education	45.00 – 50.00	45.00	55.00
Swindon College		60.00	
University of Teesside		27.00	40.00 – 55.00
Thames Valley University	80.00 – 100.00	70.00	100.00 – 110.00
Trinity College Carmarthen	76.00 – 95.00	59.00	59.00
University of Ulster		35.00	
University College London (University of London)	80.00 – 107.00	53.00	102.00 – 122.00
The University of Warwick	93.00	50.00	63.00 – 83.00
Warwickshire College, Royal Leamington Spa, Rugby and Moreton Morrell	80.00 – 100.00		
Welsh College of Horticulture		50.00	

Institution name	Cost of accommodation including meals £	Cost of accommodation with no food £	Cost of accommodation en suite, no food £
College of West Anglia	60.00 – 90.00	75.00	
University of Westminster		75.00	83.00 – 125.00
Wimbledon School of Art		80.00	
Witan International College	85.00 – 100.00	80.00	100.00 – 125.00
Wiltshire College	80.00 – 85.00		70.00
University of Wolverhampton		48.00	65.00
University College Worcester		38.00	45.00 – 48.00
Writtle College	93.00 – 100.00		
The University of York		56.00	62.00
York St John College (College of the University of Leeds)	82.00 – 86.00	49.50	62.00 – 69.00

How an average student spends money

- Socialising and entertainment £26 a week
- Books £135 a year
- Photocopying and stationery £35 a year
- Mobile phones £10 a week
- Clothing £256 a year
- Insurance £100 a year
- Internet £92 a year

Biggest outlays

After rent, most students find food is one of their biggest expenses, with the average student spending around £37 a week on food.

Weekly food spend

1. University of Bradford £88
2. University of Canterbury £78
3. Queen Mary, University of London £73
4. {King's College London £50
   {Middlesex University £50
   {Oxford Brookes University £50
   {University of Strathclyde £50
8. University of Glasgow £45
9. {Cardiff University £44
   {University of Paisley £44

| (Source: *Students' Money Matters 2004*, Gwenda Thomas, Trotman Publishing |

Leaving university with as little debt as possible

Reducing debt isn't easy, especially for those who can't rely on parents for some extra support; however, organising your finances from day one will make a massive difference.

If at all possible, try and turn up at university with some savings. That means you should start saving now. In the real world turning up at uni with savings is often not feasible, so the key is not to overspend at the beginning of the term and in the first year. It's easy to go wild in the first year, and then end up struggling to pay your excesses back until you leave university. All universities and most banks have student financial advisers: make sure you visit yours as soon as possible.

Try to use credit sensibly. Most student accounts will give you a free overdraft of around £1,000. Try to stick to this and don't go over the limit without letting your bank know. An unauthorised overdraft is like burning money in the street, as the charges are so high. What's more, your bank will send you expensive letters to let you know you've exceeded your overdraft as well. Steer clear of storecards – you often have to pay the money borrowed back at interest rates of nearly 30%. You don't have to be studying maths to work out such high interest is going to get you into trouble.

Watch out for expenses that can race out of control. Mobile phones rack up massive bills. If you can't control yourself on a contract, get a pay-as-you-go phone. Finally, if you do get into trouble, there are hardship loans that can be applied for through the university, and postgraduates such as medics can take out professional loans towards the end of their courses. But remember, everything you borrow has to be paid back. Always see if you can tighten your budget first before borrowing more money.

Follow our top tips from Julia Young, Senior Counsellor at HSBC Cardiff University so you leave uni with as little debt as possible:

Top Student Finance Tips

1. At the beginning of the year talk to a specialist adviser in a local branch. Go and meet the adviser and formulate an annual budget together.

2. Be realistic when compiling your budget – overestimate rather than underestimate your spending.

3. Keep tight control of your budget throughout the year; use your bank's online facilities to help keep track of your spending.

4. Shop around for the best student banking deal you can find. See what savings you can make – for example HSBC and NatWest offer a five-year rail card and £100.

5. Stick to your free overdraft limit and always let the bank know if you are about to exceed the limit.

6. Never use a storecard – they usually have massive APRs.

7. As soon as financial difficulty starts, go and see your bank.

8. If you do use a credit card, use it for short-term borrowing only. For example, borrow if you know your student loan is due in a couple of weeks and you will be able to pay it off. And utilise the interest-free period so you don't pay unnecessary interest.

9. Loans come in each term. Set up a savings account or ISA alongside your current account that gives you an interest rate of up to 5%, then you can transfer money into your account when you need it.

| SOURCE: HSBC |

Celebs – where they went by what they do

Want to follow in the famous footsteps of those that have made it big? Read on to see where some high achievers started out …

FUNNY GUYS

Where did comedian **Matt Lucas** of *Shooting Stars* and *Little Britain* study drama? A: Bristol

Where did **Bob Mortimer** have a laugh? A: Leicester

Where did **Ali G** study? A: Cambridge

Where did **Harry Enfield** study? A: York

Academic Ace

Where did super-brain historian **Eric Hobsbawm** develop his academic skills? A: Birkbeck

Entrepreneurs

Where did **Sahar Hashemi**, co-founder of Coffee Republic, wake up and smell the coffee? A: Bristol

Where did Easyjet founder **Stelios Haji-Ioannou** dream of becoming a successful businessman? A: City

Where did Last Minute's **Martha Lane Fox** study? A: Oxford

Where did **Tom Singh** founder of New Look go to university? A: Aberystwyth

Where did **Anita Roddick**, Body Shop founder, study? A: Bath Spa University College

Political Power

Where did **Mo Mowlam** learn to argue? A: Durham

Where did **Menzies Campbell** study? A: Glasgow

Where did **Ann Widdecombe** forge her ideas? A: Birmingham

Where did **John Prescott** and **Roy Hattersley** cut their teeth? A: Hull

Where did **Paul Boateng** study? A: Bristol

Where did **Shirley Williams** start public speaking? A: Newnham College, Cambridge

Artists and Designers

Where did **Damien Hirst, Fiona Rae, Anthony Gormley** and **Mary Quant** find their inspiration? A: Goldsmiths

Actors

Where did actress **Emily Watson** study? A: Bristol

Where did Hollywood superstar **Rachel Weisz** study? A: Trinity Hall, Cambridge

Holy man

Where did **Desmond Tutu** go to university? A: King's College London

Writers

Where did **Fay Weldon** develop her writing skills? A: St Andrews

Where did novelist **Ian McEwan** and **Peter Wilby**, editor of *The New Stateman*, write their university essays? A: Sussex

Where did **Seamus Heaney** study? A: Queen's Belfast.

Where did poet **Roger McGough** find inspiration? A: Hull

Where did **Ian Rankin** and **Sir Arthur Conan Doyle** start plotting? A: Edinburgh

Where did **Oscar Wilde** sharpen his wits? A: Magdelen College, Oxford

Where did **Deborah Maggach** study? A: Bristol

News Hounds

Where did fearless reporter **Kate Adie** study? A: Newcastle

Where did *Newsnight's* **Kirsty Wark** learn how to get to the point?
A: Edinburgh

Where did extreme interviewer **Jeremy Paxman** hone his questioning
techniques? A: St Catharine's College, Cambridge

Media Moguls

Where did **Phil Redmond**, creator of *Hollyoaks* and *Brookside*, study?
A: Liverpool

Where did **Judy Finnegan** and **Sue Lawley** study? A: Bristol

Where did **Chris Tarrant** start dreaming of his media millions? A: Birmingham

Where did **Melvyn Bragg** pursue his fascination for the arts? A: Wadham
College, Oxford

Musos

Where did the **Chemical Brothers** start mixing music? A: Manchester

Where did **Mick Jagger** tune in? A: LSE

Where did **Judge Jules** DJ in his spare time? A: LSE

Where did **Bryan Ferry** study? A: Newcastle

CHAPTER SIX

Ultimate Hobbies

University is the perfect place to develop your interests and hobbies. Getting involved will help you to meet people and find the right balance between work and extra-curricular activity.

Do our quiz and start thinking about what you couldn't live without:

Hobbies

Which of the following is you?

1) I'm a mountain man/woman: I'm only happy when I'm shinning up a steep rock face.

2) Climbing? Why would I do that when I could drive up there?

3) I'd rather stay in bed.

If rock climbing's your thing, check out the student union ratings below.

Which of the following is you?

1) There's nothing like a walk by the sea to make me feel happy.

2) I love rowing. Move over Matthew Pinsent: I'll be in the coxless fours in Beijing.

3) I'm a windsurfing fanatic.

If water gets you high, consider a university on a river or near the sea.

Which of the following is you?

1) There's nothing like an appreciative audience: I feel my best when treading the boards.

2) I've got so many ideas I must direct plays.

3) 'Ahhh the smell of greasepaint and heat of the
   light . . .'

If acting's your thing, check out the student union ratings below.

What the unions said

'Abertay Dundee is excellent for anything computer-related and sports, including Gaelic football, football and rugby.'

'The University of Wales, Aberystwyth, is excellent for many diverse sports and societies. See the full list at www.union.aber.ac.uk'

'Queen's Belfast has got 150 clubs and societies, so lots of different tastes are catered for.'

'The University of Bradford has got an excellent range of sports for students to get involved in – go to www.ubu.brad.ac.uk/sports.'

'At Bristol the students' union has over 160 societies and over 53 AU clubs, so they cater for just about everything. See www.ubu.org.uk/societies for more info.'

'Buckinghamshire Chilterns University College is good for skiing with nearby Wycombe Summit Ski slope.'

'Cambridge has an excellent range on offer. There are over 600 student-led societies in Cambridge.'

'At University of Central Lancashire (UCLAN) there are loads of skate parks. We have a climbing society and we have a campus in Cumbria with plenty of links and a wall. We have an acting degree and drama societies; we have one of the best journalism courses, an award-winning student newspaper and a journalism society. We have a huge creative writing society and have regular appearances from poets etc. We also cater for a wide variety of clubs and societies to cover all students' interests, including Gaelic football and the more unusual sports. Our sports teams are very successful and our football team are the BUSA champions. All you need to start a society is ten people.'

'Derby University is great for people interested in travel and tourism.'

'The University of East London is excellent for media interests and there are a lot of opportunities to get involved. We're starting a TV and a radio station next year. Media courses are strong in East London Uni too. Also you can start societies in anything, and in terms of culture, although the campus of East London isn't in a central bit of London, you are still in London, so you've got all of the London culture in transport distance.'

'Edge Hill College is excellent for sports.'

'With over 170 student societies to join, Edinburgh University has one of the most active student scenes in the UK and we would rate it as excellent. The university is particularly supportive of societies and acknowledges that they make a contribution to life at Edinburgh.'

'Exeter is also excellent for volunteering in the community (Community Action) and fundraising for charity through RAG (Raising and Giving).'

'Gloucestershire is also excellent for sports and societies.'

'Glasgow is also excellent for student TV and radio.'

'Liverpool John Moores has 60 clubs and societies ranging from competitive sports to drama societies.'

'Glamorgan University is excellent for surfing, sporting participation, war games, debating. A wide range of hobbies and interests are catered for. Not just your rugby and football.'

'Glasgow Caledonian has a large number of both sports and societies which have very high involvement rates, including hockey, rugby, football, trampolining.'

'Heriot-Watt is excellent for voluntary work.'

'Imperial College is excellent for media, including TV, radio and comms.'

'NUTS – Newcastle University Theatre Society – is particularly strong.'

'University College Northampton (UCN) is excellent for sports including football, rugby, golf, lacrosse, martial arts, etc.'

'For drama, journalism and music, Oxford has to be one of the best universities in the country, and there is a club for virtually every sport or hobby, and it is incredibly easy to set up new ones, both on a college and a University level – some of the university sports, football, cricket, rugby and rowing for instance, are at all-but-professional level. Student politics is also very important here, and often leads on to higher things.'

'St Andrews University is excellent for golf.'

'We've got lots of clubs and societies at Warwick University. There are 287 altogether: 77 sports clubs and 210 other societies.'

' At York, we have over 100 societies and additionally around 60 Athletic Union clubs. If you have a hobby, we cover it – if we don't, then it's easy to set up a new club/society and the Union will help fund your activities.'

To follow are the results of our student union survey on hobbies and interests. We've been a bit specific, but it should give you an idea of the range of activities you can get involved in. Go to student union websites to find out more. (See list on page 112).

Table 6.1 Student union survey on hobbies and interests

University	Windsurfing	Mountain biking	Skateboarding	Climbing	Acting	Journalism/ student newspaper	Music	Creative writing
University of Abertay Dundee	quite poor	quite poor	good	good	quite poor	quite poor	quite poor	quite poor
University of Wales, Aberystwyth	excellent	fair	fair	good	excellent	excellent	excellent	excellent
Aston University	very poor	very poor	fair	fair	fair	excellent	good	very poor
University of Wales, Bangor	excellent	excellent	good	excellent	excellent	excellent	excellent	good
Bath Spa University College	very poor	excellent	good	very poor	excellent	good	excellent	excellent
Bath University	good	excellent	excellent	good	good	good	fair	good
University of Birmingham	good*	excellent	excellent	good	excellent	excellent	excellent	fair
Bournemouth University	fair	fair	good	good	fair	excellent	good	good
University of Bradford	very poor	excellent	good	excellent	excellent	excellent	excellent	very poor
University of Bristol	good	good	fair	good	excellent	excellent	excellent	fair
Buckinghamshire Chilterns University College	n/a	n/a	good	good	good	good	fair	n/a
University of Cambridge	good	quite poor	quite poor	excellent	excellent	excellent	excellent	good
Cardiff University	excellent	good	good	good	good	excellent	good	excellent
University of Central England (UCE)	very poor	fair	good	good	fair	excellent	good	fair
University of Central Lancashire (UCLAN)	excellent	good	excellent	excellent	excellent	excellent	excellent	excellent
De Montfort University	very poor	fair	excellent	good	good	excellent	excellent	good
University of Derby	very poor	excellent	good	excellent	fair	excellent	good	good
University of Durham	fair	fair	good	good	excellent	excellent	excellent	good
University of East Anglia (UEA)	fair	quite poor	fair	good	excellent	excellent	good	excellent

University	Windsurfing	Mountain biking	Skateboarding	Climbing	Acting	Journalism/student newspaper	Music	Creative writing
University of East London	very poor	very poor	good	quite poor	good	excellent	good	very poor
Edge Hill College	quite poor	quite poor	fair	fair	excellent	good	excellent	good
University of Edinburgh	fair	good	good	excellent	excellent	excellent	excellent	excellent
University of Essex	good	quite poor	fair	excellent	good	excellent	fair	fair
University of Exeter	excellent	excellent	good	excellent	excellent	excellent	excellent	good
University of Glamorgan	quite poor	excellent	fair	excellent	good	excellent	good	excellent
University of Glasgow	quite poor	fair	quite poor	fair	excellent	excellent	good	good
Glasgow Caledonian University	fair	good	quite poor	good	quite poor	excellent	excellent	good
University of Gloucestershire	good	fair	fair	quite poor	good	excellent	fair	excellent
Heriot-Watt University	fair	quite poor	fair	good	quite poor	good	excellent	quite poor
University of Huddersfield	fair	fair	fair	good	good	excellent	excellent	fair
University of Hull	very poor	fair	fair	good	excellent	excellent	excellent	excellent
Imperial College	excellent	excellent	excellent	excellent	fair	excellent	good	quite poor
Keele University	quite poor	good	fair	good	excellent	excellent	excellent	good
University of Kent	good	fair	fair	good	excellent	good	good	fair
King's College London	good	quite poor		good	excellent	excellent	fair	quite poor
Lancaster University		excellent	fair	excellent	excellent	good	fair	fair
University of Leeds	good	good	excellent	excellent	excellent	excellent	excellent	excellent
University of Lincoln	very poor	very poor	fair	fair	fair	fair	quite poor	quite poor
University of Liverpool	good	good	very poor	good	fair	excellent	excellent	good
Liverpool Hope University								good

College	Windsurfing	Mountain biking	Skateboarding	Climbing	Acting	Journalism/student newspaper	Music	Creative writing
Liverpool John Moores University	quite poor	fair	quite poor	fair	good	fair	good	good
London Metropolitan University	quite poor	fair	fair	excellent	excellent	excellent	excellent	good
London School of Economics and Political Science (LSE)	good	good	fair	excellent	good	excellent	fair	good
Loughborough University	very poor	very poor	very poor	fair	good	excellent	good	good
Manchester Metropolitan University	good	n/a	n/a	excellent	n/a	fair	fair	fair
University of Newcastle	excellent	excellent	good	excellent	excellent	excellent	excellent	good
University College Northampton (UCN)	quite poor	quite poor	quite poor	quite poor	good	good	excellent	good
University of Oxford	excellent	excellent	excellent	excellent	excellent	excellent	excellent	fair
Oxford Brookes University	very poor	quite poor	quite poor	excellent	good	excellent	excellent	excellent
University of Paisley	quite poor	excellent	fair	excellent	good	good	excellent	good
University of Plymouth	excellent	fair	excellent	good	good	very poor	fair	good
University of Portsmouth	excellent	good	excellent	good	fair	excellent	excellent	fair
Queen's University Belfast	good	good	good	excellent	excellent	excellent	excellent	excellent
University of Reading	fair	very poor	fair	fair	good	good	good	fair
Royal Holloway, University of London	quite poor	fair	good	excellent	excellent	excellent	excellent	good
University of St Andrews	good	good	fair	good	excellent	excellent	good	excellent
University of Sheffield	fair	excellent	excellent	excellent	excellent	excellent	excellent	excellent

University	Windsurfing	Mountain biking	Skateboarding	Climbing	Acting	Journalism/ student newspaper	Music	Creative writing
Sheffield Hallam University	quite poor	excellent	good	excellent	fair	fair	good	good
University of Southampton	excellent	good	quite poor	good	excellent	excellent	good	fair
Southampton Institute	excellent	good	good	good	fair	good	good	good
University of Sunderland	fair	good	good	good	excellent	excellent	good	fair
University of Sussex	good	good	fair		excellent	excellent	good	excellent
University of Surrey	fair	good	quite poor	excellent	excellent	excellent	excellent	fair
University of Wales, Swansea	excellent	good	good	good	good	excellent	good	good
University of Warwick	excellent	excellent	fair	excellent	excellent	excellent	excellent	fair
University of Wolverhampton	very poor	fair	good	good	excellent	excellent	good	good
University of York	excellent	excellent	excellent	excellent	excellent	excellent	excellent	excellent

Which universities cater best for your favourite hobby? These are some of the self-confessed best and worst:

Acting excellent

University of Wales, Bangor; University of Birmingham; University of Bradford; University of Cambridge; University of Central Lancashire (UCLAN); University of Derby; University of Edinburgh; University of Exeter; University of Glamorgan; Imperial College London; Keele University; Lancaster University; University of Leeds; Liverpool John Moores University; London Metropolitan University; Loughborough University; University of Newcastle; Oxford Brookes University; Queen's University, Belfast; Royal Holloway, University of London; University of Sheffield; Sheffield Hallam University; University of Surrey; University of Warwick; University of York.

Acting quite poor

University of Abertay, Dundee; Glasgow Caledonian University; Heriot-Watt University.

Journalism/student newspaper excellent

University of Wales, Aberystwyth; Aston University; University of Wales, Bangor; University of Birmingham; Bournemouth University; University of Bradford; University of Bristol; University of Cambridge; University of Cardiff; University of Central England (UCE); University of Central Lancashire (UCLAN); De Montfort University; University of Derby; University of Durham; University of East Anglia (UEA); University of East London; University of Edinburgh; University of Exeter; University of Glamorgan; University of Glasgow; Glasgow Caledonian University; University of Gloucestershire; University of Huddersfield; University of Hull; Imperial College London; Keele University; King's College London; University of Leeds; University of Liverpool; Liverpool John Moores University; London Metropolitan University; London School of Economics and Political Science (LSE); Manchester Metropolitan University; University of Newcastle; Oxford Brookes University; University of Portsmouth; Queen's University Belfast; Royal Holloway, University of London; University of St Andrews; University of Sheffield; University of Sunderland; University of Surrey; University of Sussex; University of Wales, Swansea; University of Warwick; University of York.

Journalism/student newspaper poor

University of Abertay Dundee; University of Plymouth.

If you want to be a journalist, it's a good idea to get some experience while you're at university. Remember you can always turn round an existing paper or magazine or start your own. But just so you know, these are the universities that already have a strong output.

NUS and the Daily Mirror National Student Journalism Awards 2003

Category one – Best Student Newspaper

Winner: *York Vision*, University of York

Category two – Best Student Magazine

Winner: *Pugwash*, Portsmouth University

Category three – Best Small Budget Student Publication

Winner: *Fuel*, University of East London

Category four – Best Student Media Website

Winner: *Durham21*, Durham University

Category five – Best Further Education Publication

Winner: *BritSprog*, Broxtowe College

| **Source:** nus.org.uk |

I WISH I'D GOT MORE INVOLVED

'I wish I'd known how easy it is to get involved in all aspects of the Students' Union from the moment I arrived.' – Student from Royal Holloway, University of London.

'I wish I could have realised earlier on in my university life how many opportunities there are for students here, from internships to societies offering a huge variety of interests. I only began to get heavily involved in my third year, when I should have been concentrating on my studies.' – Student from St Andrews.

'I wish I'd realised the opportunities to expand my CV and meet new people by getting involved in the Students' Union. I didn't get involved until the end of my degree, but would have wanted to do things from day one really.' – Student from Liverpool Hope University College.

'I should have found out that the SU did more than just run the bar ... I'd have got involved sooner, and enjoyed myself even more than I did!' – Student from Buckinghamshire Chilterns University College.

Music excellent

University of Wales, Aberystwyth; University of Wales, Bangor; Bath Spa University College; University of Birmingham; University of Bradford; University of Bristol; University of Cambridge; University of Central Lancashire (UCLAN); De Montfort University; University of Durham; Edge Hill College; University of Edinburgh; University of Exeter; Heriot-Watt University; University of Huddersfield; University of Hull; Keele University; University of Leeds; University of Liverpool; Liverpool John Moores University; University of Newcastle Upon Tyne; University College Northampton (UCN); Oxford Brookes University; University of Portsmouth; Queen's University, Belfast; Royal Holloway, University of London; University of Sheffield; University of Surrey; University of Warwick; University of York.

Music quite poor

Abertay Dundee University; University of Lincoln.

Creative writing excellent

University of Wales, Aberystwyth; Bath Spa University College; Cardiff University; University of Central Lancashire (UCLAN); University of East Anglia (UEA); University of Edinburgh; University of Glamorgan; University of Gloucestershire; University of Hull; University of Leeds; University of Portsmouth University of St Andrews; University of Sheffield; University of York.

Creative writing poor

University of Abertay Dundee; University of Bradford; King's College London.

Windsurfing excellent

University of Wales, Aberystwyth; University of Wales, Bangor; Cardiff University; University of Central Lancashire (UCLAN); University of Exeter; Imperial College London; University of Newcastle; University of Plymouth; University of Portsmouth; University of Wales, Swansea; University of Warwick; University of York.

Windsurfing very poor

Aston University; Bath Spa University College; University of Bradford; University of Central England (UCE); De Montfort University; University of Derby; University of East London; University of Hull; University of Lincoln; London School of Economics and Political Science (LSE); Oxford Brookes University; University of Wolverhampton.

Mountain biking excellent

University of Wales, Bangor; Bath Spa University College; University of Birmingham; University of Bradford; University of Derby; University of Exeter; University of Glamorgan; Imperial College London; Lancaster University; University of Newcastle; University of Sheffield; Sheffield Hallam University; University of Warwick; University of York.

Mountain biking very poor

Aston University; University of East London; London School of Economics and Political Science (LSE).

Skateboarding excellent

University of Bath; University of Birmingham; University of Central Lancashire (UCLAN); De Montfort University; Imperial College London; University of Leeds; University of Plymouth; University of Portsmouth; University of Sheffield; University of York.

Skateboarding quite poor

University of Cambridge; University of Glasgow; Glasgow Caledonian University; University of Liverpool; Liverpool Hope University College; London School of Economics and Political Science (LSE); Oxford Brookes University; University College Northampton (UCN); University of Surrey.

Climbing excellent

University of Wales, Bangor; University of Bradford; University of Cambridge; University of Central Lancashire (UCLAN); University of Derby; University of Edinburgh; University of Exeter; University of Glamorgan; Imperial College London; Lancaster University; University of Leeds; Liverpool John Moores University College; London Metropolitan University; Loughborough University; Manchester Metropolitan University; University of Newcastle; Oxford Brookes University; Queen's University, Belfast; Roehampton University of Surrey; Royal Holloway, University of London; University of Sheffield; Sheffield Hallam University; University of Surrey; University of York.

Climbing poor

University of East London; University of Gloucestershire; University College Northampton.

I WISH I'D KNOWN . . .

'... how expensive Oxford is, how pretentious some people can be and how many beggars there are!' – Student from Oxford Brookes University.

I WISH I'D KNOWN . . .

'... how good Plymouth was.' – Student from Plymouth.

Quizmasters

When you do become a super-brainy student, what better way to display your knowledge than to join your university's quiz team? And everyone knows the holy grail of the university quiz team is the long-running TV show, *University Challenge* where students get Paxoed by the tough-talking Jeremy Paxman.

If you do ever make it on to TV's *University Challenge* you will be following in the footsteps of some famous names, including **Clive James**, **David Mellor**, **Stephen Fry**, **John Simpson** and **Malcolm Rifkind**.

Magdalen College, Oxford are the *University Challenge* quiz masters, having won the competition three times, including the 2004 title.

University Challenge Series Champions

Original Series; presenter, Bamber Gascoigne
1963	University of Leicester
1965	New College, Oxford
1966	Oriel College, Oxford
1967	University of Sussex
1968	Keele University
1969	University of Sussex
1970	Churchill College, Cambridge
1971	Sidney Sussex College, Cambridge
1972	University College, Oxford
1973	Fitzwilliam College, Cambridge
1974	Trinity College, Cambridge
1975	Keble College, Oxford
1976	University College, Oxford
1977	University of Durham
1978	Sidney Sussex College, Cambridge
1979	University of Bradford
1980	Merton College, Oxford
1981	Queen's University, Belfast
1982	University of St Andrews
1983	University of Dundee
1984	Open University

1986	Jesus College, Oxford
1987	Keble College, Oxford

New Series; presenter, Jeremy Paxman

1995	Trinity College, Cambridge
1996	Imperial College, London
1997	Magdalen College, Oxford
1998	Magdalen College, Oxford
1999	Open University
2000	University of Durham
2001	Imperial College, London
2002	Somerville College, Oxford
2003	Birkbeck College, London
2004	Magdalen College, Oxford

| **SOURCE:** Department of Applied Mathematics and Theoretical Physics website, University of Cambridge. Go to www.damtp.cam.ac.uk |

Sport at university

'Getting involved in sport at university couldn't be easier! The British Universities Sports Association (BUSA) works in conjunction with athletic unions and sports offices all over the country, so just pop into your students' union and ask to see the officer responsible for sport. University sport has both breadth and depth, so whatever your level and whatever your sport, you can take part.' G.Gregory Jones, Chief Executive, BUSA

I WISH I'D KNOWN . . .

'... that everyone else here is very, very attractive. That has its upsides as well though!' – Student from Loughborough University.

BUSA University Championship Competition 2003/4

1. **Loughborough University**

2. **University of Bath**

3. **University of Birmingham**

4. **University of Nottingham**

5. University of Cambridge

6. University of Exeter

7. University of Wales Institute, Cardiff

8. University of Edinburgh

9. University of Oxford

10. University of Durham

11. University of Manchester

12. University of Leeds

13. University of Bristol

14. Cardiff University

15. Northumbria University

16. University of Southampton

17. Sheffield Hallam University

18. University of Stirling

19. University of Newcastle

20. University of Warwick

21. London Metropolitan University

22. Brunel University

23. University of London

24. University of Glasgow

25. University of Brighton

26. University of Aberdeen

27. Leeds Metropolitan University

28. St Mary's College

29. College of St Mark and St John

29. University College London

31. Nottingham Trent University

32. University of Sheffield

32. University of St Andrews

34. University of Kent

35. London South Bank University

36. University of Strathclyde

37. Oxford Brookes University

38. University of Liverpool

39. Southampton Institute

40. London School of Economics

41. Crewe and Alsager, Cheshire

42. Heriot-Watt University

43. Middlesex University

44. Imperial College London

45. University of Portsmouth

46. Liverpool John Moores University

47. University of Reading

48. University College Worcester

49. University of Gloucestershire

50. University of Wales, Swansea

51. Lancaster University

52. University of York

53. University of Bournemouth

54. Chichester University College

55. University of Dundee

56. University of Plymouth

57. University of Sussex

57. University of East Anglia

59. University of Central Lancashire

60. University of Wales, Aberystwyth

61. University of Coventry

62. University of Teesside

62. Queen Mary, University of London

64. University of Manchester Institute of Science and Technology

65. Royal Agricultural College

66. University of Glamorgan

67. Edge Hill College

67. King's College London

69. University of Surrey

70. Staffordshire University

71. University College Chester

72. University of Hull

73. **Manchester Metropolitan University**

74. **University of Hertfordshire**

75. **University of West of England**

75. **University of Wales, Cardiff Medics**

77. **Liverpool Hope University College**

78. **Queen's Belfast University**

79. **Hartpury College**

80. **University of Sunderland**

81. **Robert Gordon University**

82. **Kingston University**

82. **Harper Adams University College**

84. **University of Salford**

85. **University of Abertay Dundee**

86. **Buckinghamshire Chilterns University College**

86. **University of Lincoln (Lincoln)**

88. **University of Leicester**

88. **Glasgow Caledonian University**

90. **De Montfort University**

90. **University of Essex**

92. **University of Derby**

93. **Guy's, King's and St Thomas'**

94. **University of Wales, Bangor**

94. **University of Greenwich**

96. **Royal Holloway University of London**

97. **Keele University**

98. **University of Ulster**

98. **University of Bradford**

98. **Napier University**

98. **Trinity and All Saints**

98. **De Montfort University**

103. **Canterbury Christ Church University College**

104. **University of Huddersfield**

105. **University of York**

106. **Royal Veterinary College**

107. **University College Northampton**

108. **Royal Free and University College Medics**

109. **St Martins College**

110. **Roehampton University**

110. **University of Wolverhampton**

112. **University of Central England**

113. **Bolton Institute of Higher Education**

114. **University of Luton**

114. **Swansea Institute**

114. **University of Westminster**

114. **Cranfield University (Bedfordshire)**

118. **Aston University**

118. **North East Wales Institute**

120. **Writtle College**

| **Source:** British Universities Sports Association BUSA |

CHAPTER SEVEN

Your Own Ultimate Research

And now it's up to you to do your own ultimate research. We hope you've got some good leads and ideas from this book and wish you luck getting a place at your chosen university. Get your checklist at the ready and get researching.

The information

Student union websites

Aberdeen University Students' Association www.ausa.org.uk

Abertay Students' Association www.abertayunion.com

Aberystwyth Guild of Students www.union.aber.ac.uk

Anglia Polytechnic University Students' Union www.apusu.com

Aston Students' Guild www.astonguild.org.uk

Bangor Students' Union www.undeb.bangor.ac.uk

Bath Students' Union www.bathstudent.com

Birmingham Guild of Students www.bugs.bham.ac.uk

Bournemouth Students' Union www.subu.org.uk

Bradford Students' Union www.ubu.brad.ac.uk

Brighton Students' Union www.ubsu.net

Bristol Union www.ubu.org.uk

Brunel Students' Union www.brunelstudents.com

Cambridge Students' Union www.cusu.cam.ac.uk

Cardiff Students' Union www.cardiffstudents.com

Cardiff UWIC Student Union www.uwicsu.co.uk

Central England Union of Students www.unionofstudents.com

Central Lancashire Student Union www.yourunion.co.uk

City Students' Union www.cusuonline.org

Coventry Students' Union www.cusu.org

De Montfort Students' Union www.mydsu.com

Derby Students' Union www.udsu-online.co.uk

Dundee University Students' Association www.dusa.dundee.ac.uk

Durham Students' Union www.dsu.org.uk

East Anglia Students' Union www.stu.uea.ac.uk

East London's Students' Union www.uelsu.net

Edinburgh Students' Association www.eusa.ed.ac.uk

Essex Students' Union www.essexstudent.com

Exeter Guild of Students www.xnet.ex.ac.uk

Glamorgan Students' Union www.glamsu.com

Glasgow Students' Representative Council www.glasgowstudent.net

Glasgow Caledonian Students' Association www.caledonianstudent.com

Gloucestershire Students' Union www.ugsu.org

Goldsmiths Students' Union www.gcsu.org.uk

Greenwich Students' Union www.suug.co.uk

Heriot-Watt Students' Association www.hwusa.org

Hertfordshire Students' Union www.uhsu.herts.ac.uk

Huddersfield Students' Union www.huddersfieldstudent.com

Hull Students' Union www.hullstudent.com

Imperial College Students' Union www.union.ic.ac.uk

Keele Students' Union www.kusu.net

Kent Students' Union www.kentunion.co.uk

King's College London Students' Union www.kclsu.og

Kingston Students' Union www.kingston.ac.uk/guild

Lampeter Students' Union www.lamp.ac.uk/su

Lancaster Students' Union www.lusu.co.uk

Leeds University Union www.luuonline.com

Leeds Metropolitan Students' Union www.lmusu.org.uk

Leicester Students' Union www.leicesterstudent.org

Lincoln Students' Union www.lincolnsu.com

Liverpool Guild of Students www.liverpoolguild.org.uk

Liverpool John Moores Students' Union www.l-s-u.com

University of London Students' Union www.ulucube.com

London Metropolitan Students' Union www.londonmetsu.org.uk

London School of Economics Students' Union www.lsesu.com

London South Bank Students' Union www.lsbsu.org

Loughborough Students' Union www.lufbra.net

Luton Student Union www.ulsu.net

Manchester University www.umu.man.ac.uk

UMIST www.su.umist.ac.uk

(soon to merge into www.manchesterstudents.org)

Manchester Metropolitan Students' Union www.mmsu.com

Middlesex Students' Union www.musu.mdx.ac.uk

Napier Students' Association www.napierstudents.com

Newcastle Union Society www.unionsociety.co.uk

Newport Students' Union www.newportunion.com

Northumbria Students' Union www.mynsu.co.uk

Nottingham Students' Union www.students-union.nottingham.ac.uk

Nottingham Trent Union of Students www.su.ntu.ac.uk

Oxford Students' Union www.ousu.org

Oxford Brookes Students' Union www.thesu.com

Paisley Students' Association www.upsa.org.uk

Plymouth Students' Union www.upsuonline.co.uk

Portsmouth Students' Union www.upsu.net

Queen Mary Students' Union www.qmsu.org

Queen's Belfast Students' Union www.qubsu.org

Reading Students' Union www.rusu.co.uk

Robert Gordon Student Association www.rgunion.co.uk

Royal Holloway Students' Union www.su.rhul.ac.uk

St Andrews Students' Association www.yourunion.net

Salford Students' Union www.susu.salford.ac.uk

SOAS Students' Union www.soasunion.org

Sheffield Union of Students www.sheffieldunion.com

Sheffield Hallam Students' Union www.hallamunion.com

Southampton Students' Union www.susu.org

Staffordshire Students' Union www.staffsunion.com

Stirling Students' Association www.susaonline.org.uk

Strathclyde Students' Association www.strathstudents.com

Sunderland Students' Union www.sunderlandsu.co.uk

Surrey Students' Union www.ussu.co.uk

Surrey Roehampton Students' Union www.roehamptonstudent.com

Sussex Students' Union www.ussu.info

Swansea Students' Union www.swansea-union.co.uk

Teesside Students' Union www.utu.org.uk

Thames Valley Students' Union www.tvusu.org.uk

Ulster Students' Union www.uusu.org

University College London Students' Union www.uclu.org

University of the Arts, London Students' Union www.lisu.org

Warwick Students' Union www.sunion.warwick.ac.uk/portal

West of England Students' Union www.uwsu.com

Wolverhampton Students' Union www.wolvesunion.org

York Students' Union www.yusu.org

Useful Contacts

Department for Education and Skills
DSA Information
Student Support Division 1
2F Area C
Mowden Hall
Staindrop Road
Darlington
DL3 9BG

Tel: 01325 392822
Website:
www.dfes.gsi.gov.uk/studentssupport

Department of Education for
Northern Ireland
Rathgael House
43 Balloo Road
Bangor
County Down
BT19 7 PR

Tel: 028 9127 9100
Website: www.deni.gov.uk

National Union of Students (NUS)
Nelson Mandela House
461 Holloway Road
London N7 6 LJ

Tel: 020 7272 8900
Website: www.nusonline.co.uk

Student Loans Company Limited
100 Bothwell Street
Glasgow
G2 7JD

Tel: 0800 40 50 10
Website: www.slc.co.uk

UCAS
Rosehill
New Barn Lane
Cheltenham
Gloucestershire
GL52 3LZ

Tel: 01242 222444
Website: www.ucas.ac.uk

Institution contact details

The University of Aberdeen
University Office
King's College
Aberdeen
AB24 3FX

Tel: 01224 273504
Website: www.abdn.ac.uk/sras

University of Abertay Dundee
Bell Street
Dundee
DD1 1HG

Tel: 01382 308080
Website: www.abertay.ac.uk

The University of Wales, Aberystwyth
Old College
King Street
Aberystwyth
SY23 2AX

Tel: 01970 622021
Website: www.aber.ac.uk

Anglia Polytechnic University
Bishop Hall Lane
Chelmsford
CM1 1SQ

Tel: 0845 271 3333
Website: www.apu.ac.uk

Aston University
Aston Triangle
Birmingham
B4 7ET

Tel: 0121 359 6313
Website: www.aston.ac.uk

University of Wales, Bangor
Bangor
Gwynedd
LL57 2DG

Tel: 01248 382016/2017/2018
Website: www.bangor.ac.uk

University of Bath
Claverton Down
Bath
BA2 7AY

Tel: 01225 383019
Website: www.bath.ac.uk

Bath Spa University College
Newton Park
Newton St Loe
Bath
BA2 9BN

Tel: 01225 875875
Website: www.bathspa.ac.uk

The University of Birmingham
Edgbaston
Birmingham
B15 2TT

Tel: 0121 414 5491
Website: www.bham.ac.uk

Bolton Institute of Higher Education
Deane Road
Bolton
BL3 5AB

Tel: 01204 528851/900600
Website: www.bolton.ac.uk

Bournemouth University
Talbot Campus
Fern Barrow
Poole
BH12 5BB

Tel: 01202 524111
Website: www.bournemouth.ac.uk

The University of Bradford
Richmond Road
Bradford
West Yorkshire
BD7 1DP

Tel: 01274 233081
Website: www.bradford.ac.uk

University of Brighton
Mithras House
Lewes Road
Brighton
BN2 4AT

Tel: 01273 600900
Website: www.brighton.ac.uk

Brighton and Sussex Medical School
University of Brighton
Mithras House
Lewes Road
BN2 4AT

Tel: 01273 600900
Website: www.bsms.ac.uk

University of Bristol
Undergraduate Admissions Office
Senate House
Tyndall Avenue
BS8 1TH

Tel: 0117 928 9000
Website: www.bris.ac.uk

Bristol Filton College
Filton Avenue
BS34 7AT

Tel: 0117 931 2121
Website: www.filton.ac.uk

University of the West of England,
Bristol
Frenchay Campus
Coldharbour Lane
Bristol
BS16 1QY

Tel: 0117 328 3333
Website: www.uwe.ac.uk

Brunel University
Uxbridge
Middlesex
UB8 3PH

Tel: 01895 203214
Website: www.brunel.ac.uk

The University of Buckingham
Hunter Street
Buckingham
MK18 1EG

Tel: 01280 814080
Website: www.buckingham.ac.uk

Buckinghamshire Chilterns University
College
Queen Alexandra Road
High Wycombe
Bucks
HP11 2JZ

Tel: 01494 522141
Website: www.bcuc.ac.uk

University of Cambridge
Cambridge Admissions Office
Kellet Lodge
Tennis Court Road
CB2 1QT

Tel: 01223 333308
Website: www.cam.ac.uk

Canterbury Christ Church University
College
Canterbury
Kent
CT1 1QU

Tel: 01227 782900
Website: www.canterbury.ac.uk

Cardiff University
PO Box 927
50 Park Place
Cardiff
CF10 3UA

Tel: 029 2087 4404
Website: www.cardiff.ac.uk

University of Wales Institute, Cardiff
PO Box 377
Llandaff Campus
Western Avenue
CF5 2SG

Tel: 029 2041 6070
Website: www.uwic.ac.uk

University of Central England in
Birmingham
Perry Barr
Birmingham
B42 2SU

Tel: 0121 331 5000
Website: www.uce.ac.uk

University of Central Lancashire
Preston
Lancashire
PRI 2HE

Tel: 01772 201201
Website: www.uclan.ac.uk

University College Chester
Parkgate Road
Chester
CHI 4BJ

Tel: 01244 375444
Website: www.chester.ac.uk

City University
Northampton Square
London
ECIV 0HB

Tel: 020 7040 5060
Website: www.city.ac.uk

Colchester Institute
Sheepen Road
Colchester
Essex
CO3 3LL

Tel: 01206 518777
Website: www.colchester.ac.uk

Courtauld Institute of Art (University
of London)
Somerset House
Strand
London
WC2R 0RN

Tel: 020 7848 2645
Website: www.courtauld.ac.uk

Coventry University
Priory Street
Coventry
CVI 5FB

Tel: 0845 055 5850
Website: www.coventry.ac.uk

Dartington College of Arts
Registry
Totnes
TQ9 6EJ

Tel: 01803 861620
Website: www.dartington.ac.uk

De Montfort University
The Gateway
Leicester
LEI 9BH

Tel: 0116 255 1551
Website: www.dmu.ac.uk

University of Derby
Kedleston Road
Derby
DE22 1GB

Tel: 08701 202330
Website: www.derby.ac.uk

University of Dundee
Dundee
DD1 4HN

Tel: 01382 344160
Website: www.dundee.ac.uk

The University of Durham
University Office
Durham
DH1 3HP

Tel: 0191 334 2000
Website: www.dur.ac.uk

The University of East Anglia
Norwich
NR4 7TJ

Tel: 01603 456161
Website: www.uea.ac.uk

University of East London
Barking Campus
Longbridge Road
Dagenham
RM8 2AS

Tel: 020 8223 2835
Website: www.uel.ac.uk

Edge Hill College of Higher Education
Ormskirk
Lancashire
L39 4QP

Tel: 0800 195 5063
Website: www.edgehill.ac.uk

The University of Edinburgh
Recruitment & Admissions Liaison
Service
57 George Square
Edinburgh
EH8 9JU

Tel: 0131 650 4360
Website: www.ed.ac.uk

Edinburgh College of Art
74 Lauriston Place
EH3 9DF

Tel: 0131 221 6027
Website: www.eca.ac.uk

The University of Essex
Wivenhoe Park
Colchester
CO4 3SQ

Tel: 01206 873666
Website: www.essex.ac.uk

European Business School, London
EBS London
Regent's College
Regent's Park
NW1 4NS

Tel: 020 7487 7505
Website: www.ebslondon.ac.uk

University of Exeter
The Queen's Drive
Exeter
EX4 4QJ

Tel: 01392 263035
Website: www.ex.ac.uk

University of Glamorgan
ADMAIL 3541
Pontypridd
Mid Glamorgan
CF37 1GY

Tel: 0800 716925
Website: www.glam.ac.uk

University of Glasgow
The University
Glasgow
G12 8QQ

Tel: 0141 330 4575
Website: www.gla.ac.uk

Glasgow Caledonian University
City Campus
Cowcaddens Road
Glasgow
G4 0BA

Tel: 0141 331 3000
Website: www.gcal.ac.uk

The Glasgow School of Art
167 Renfrew Street
Glasgow
G3 6RQ

Tel: 0141 353 4512
Website: www.gsa.ac.uk

The University of Gloucestershire
Hardwick Campus
St Paul's Road
Cheltenham
GL50 4BS

Tel: 01242 532825
Website: www.glos.ac.uk

Goldsmiths College (University of
London)
Lewisham Way
New Cross
London
SE14 6NW

Tel: 020 7919 7766
Website: www.goldsmiths.ac.uk

University of Greenwich
Maritime Greenwich Campus
Old Royal Naval College
Park Row
SE10 9LS

Tel: 0800 005 006
Website: www.gre.ac.uk

Harper Adams University College
Newport
Shropshire
TF10 8NB

Tel: 01952 820280
Website: www.harper-adams.ac.uk

Heriot-Watt University
Edinburgh Campus
Edinburgh
EH14 4AS

Tel: 0131 449 5111
Website: www.hw.ac.uk

University of Hertfordshire
University Admissions Service
College Lane
Hatfield
AL10 9AB

Tel: 01707 284800
Website: www.herts.ac.uk

Heythrop College (University of
London)
Kensington Square
London
W8 5HQ

Tel: 020 7795 6600
Website: www.heythrop.ac.uk

The University of Huddersfield
Queensgate
Huddersfield
HD1 3DH

Tel: 01484 422288
Website: www.hud.ac.uk

The University of Hull
Hull
HU6 7RX

Tel: 01482 466100
Website: www.hull.ac.uk

Hull York Medical School
HYMS Admissions Section
Admissions & Schools Liaison
University of York
YO10 5DD

Tel: 0870 120 2323
Website: www.hyms.ac.uk

Imperial College London (University of
London)
Registry: Admissions
South Kensington Campus
Imperial College London
SW7 2AZ

Tel: 020 7594 8001
Website: www.imperial.ac.uk

Keele University
Keele
Staffs
ST5 5BG

Tel: 01782 584005
Website: www.keele.ac.uk

The University of Kent
Information, Recruitment & Admissions
Registry
University of Kent
CT2 7NZ

Tel: 01227 827272
Website: www.kent.ac.uk

Kent Institute of Art and Design
Registry – Admissions
Fort Pitt
Rochester
ME1 1DZ

Tel: 01634 888773
Website: www.kiad.ac.uk

King Alfred's Winchester
Winchester
Hampshire
SO22 4NR

Tel: 01962 827234
Website: www.wkac.ac.uk

King's College London (University of
London)
Strand
London
WC2R 2LS

Tel: 020 7836 5454
Website: www.kcl.ac.uk

Kingston University
Student Information & Advice Centre
Cooper House
40–46 Surbiton Road
KT1 2HX

Tel: 020 8547 7053
Website: www.kingston.ac.uk

Lampeter, The University of Wales
Admissions Office
University of Wales
Lampeter
SA48 7ED

Tel: 01570 422351
Website: www.lamp.ac.uk

Lancaster University
Lancaster
Lancashire
LA1 4YW

Tel: 01524 65201
Website: www.lancs.ac.uk

University of Leeds
Leeds
LS2 9JT

Tel: 0113 343 3999
Website: www.leeds.ac.uk

Leeds Trinity and All Saints (Accredited
College of the University of Leeds)
Brownberrie Lane
Horsforth
Leeds
LS18 5HD

Tel: 0113 283 7123
Website: www.tasc.ac.uk

Leeds Metropolitan University
Course Enquiries Office
City Campus
Leeds
LS1 3HE

Tel: 0113 283 3113
Website: www.leedsmet.ac.uk

Leeds College of Art and Design
Blenheim Walk
Leeds
LS2 9AQ

Tel: 0113 202 8000
Website: www.leeds-art.ac.uk

Leeds College of Music
3 Quarry Hill
Leeds
West Yorkshire
LS2 7PD
Tel: 0113 222 3416
Website: www.lcm.ac.uk

University of Leicester
University Road
Leicester
LE1 7RH

Tel: 0116 252 5281
Website: www.le.ac.uk

University of Lincoln
Admissions & Customer Services
Brayford Pool
LN6 7TS

Tel: 01522 886097
Website: www.lincoln.ac.uk

The University of Liverpool
Senate House
Abercromby Square
Liverpool
L69 3BX

Tel: 0151 794 2000
Website: www.liv.ac.uk

Liverpool Hope University College
Hope Park
Liverpool
L16 9JD

Tel: 0151 291 3295
Website: www.hope.ac.uk

Liverpool John Moores University
Roscoe Court
4 Rodney Street
Liverpool
L1 2TZ

Tel: 0151 231 5090
Website: www.jmu.ac.uk

The London Institute
65 Davies Street
London
W1K 5DA

Tel: 020 7514 6000 x6197
Website: www.linst.ac.uk

London Metropolitan University
166–220 Holloway Road
London
N7 8DB

Tel: 020 7133 4200
Website: www.londonmet.ac.uk

London School of Economics and
Political Science (University of London)
PO Box 13401
Houghton Street
London
WC2A 2AS

Tel: 020 7955 7125/7769
Website: www.lse.ac.uk

London South Bank University
103 Borough Road
London
SE1 0AA

Tel: 020 7815 7815
Website: www.lsbu.ac.uk

Loughborough University
Loughborough
Leicestershire
LE11 3TU

Tel: 01509 263171
Website: www.lboro.ac.uk

University of Luton
Park Square
Luton
Beds
LU1 3JU

Tel: 01582 489286
Website: www.luton.ac.uk

The University of Manchester
Oxford Road
Manchester
M13 9PL

Tel: 0161 275 2077
Website: www.manchester.ac.uk

The University of Manchester Institute
of Science and Technology (UMIST)
PO Box 88
Manchester
M60 1QD

Tel: 0161 200 4034
Website: www.umist.ac.uk

The Manchester Metropolitan
University
Admissions Office
All Saints
Manchester
M15 6BH

Tel: 0161 247 2000
Website: www.mmu.ac.uk

The College of St Mark and St John
Derriford Road
Plymouth
PL6 8BH

Tel: 01752 636890
Website: www.marjon.ac.uk

Middlesex University
North London Business Park
Oakleigh Road South
London
N11 1QS

Tel: 020 8411 5898
Website: www.mdx.ac.uk

Myerscough College
Myerscough Hall
Bilsborrow
PR3 0RY

Tel: 01995 642222
Website: www.myerscough.ac.uk

Napier University, Edinburgh
10 Colinton Road
Edinburgh
EH10 5DT

Tel: 0500 353570
Website: www.napier.ac.uk

University of Newcastle Upon Tyne
6 Kensington Terrace
Newcastle upon Tyne
NE1 7RU

Tel: 0191 222 5594
Website: www.ncl.ac.uk

Newport, University of Wales
Caerleon Campus
PO Box 101
Newport
NP18 3YH

Tel: 01633 432030
Website: www.newport.ac.uk

University College Northampton
Park Campus
Boughton Green Road
Northampton
NN2 7AL

Tel: 0800 358 2232
Website: www.northampton.ac.uk

The Norwich School of Art and
Design
St George Street
Norwich
Norfolk
NR3 1BB

Tel: 01603 610561
Website: www.nsad.ac.uk

Northumbria University
Ellison Building
Ellison Place
Newcastle upon Tyne
NE1 8ST

Tel: 0191 232 6002
Website: www.northumbria.ac.uk

Norwich City College of Further and
Higher Education (a regional college of
Anglia Polytechnic University)
Ipswich Road
Norwich
Norfolk
NR2 2LJ

Tel: 01603 773136
Website: www.ccn.ac.uk

The University of Nottingham
The Admissions Office
E Floor, Portland Building
University of Nottingham
NG7 2RD

Tel: 0115 951 5151
Website: www.nottingham.ac.uk

The Nottingham Trent University
Burton Street
Nottingham
NG1 4BU

Tel: 0115 941 8418
Website: www.ntu.ac.uk

University of Oxford
Oxford Colleges Admissions Office
Wellington Square
Oxford
OX1 2JD

Tel: 01865 288000
Website: www.admissions.ox.ac.uk

Oxford Brookes University
Admissions Office
Gipsy Lane Campus
Headington
OX3 0BP

Tel: 01865 483040
Website: www.brookes.ac.uk

University of Paisley
Paisley
Renfrewshire
Scotland
PA1 2BE

Tel: 0141 848 3727
Website: www.paisley.ac.uk

Pembrokeshire College (accredited
college of University of Glamorgan)
Haverfordwest
Pembrokeshire
SA61 1SZ

Tel: 01437 765247
Website: www.pembrokeshire.ac.uk

Peninsula Medical School
ITTC Building
Tamar Science Park
Derriford
PL6 8BX

Tel: 01752 764439
Website: www.pms.ac.uk

University of Plymouth
Drake Circus
Plymouth
PL4 8AA

Tel: 01752 232137
Website: www.plymouth.ac.uk

University of Portsmouth
Academic Registry
University House
Winston Churchill Avenue
PO1 2UP

Tel: 023 9284 8484
Website: www.port.ac.uk

Queen Margaret University College,
Edinburgh
Clerwood Terrace
Edinburgh
EH12 8TS

Tel: 0131 317 3247
Website: www.qmuc.ac.uk

Queen Mary, University of London
Mile End Road
London
E1 4NS

Tel: 020 7882 5555
Website: www.qmul.ac.uk

Queen's University Belfast
University Road
Belfast
BT7 1NN

Tel: 028 9097 5081
Website: www.qub.ac.uk/

The University of Reading
PO Box 217
Reading
RG6 6AH

Tel: 0118 987 5123
Website: www.rdg.ac.uk

Regents Business School London
Regent's College
Inner Circle
Regent's Park
NW1 4NS

Tel: 020 7487 7654
Website: www.RBSLondon.ac.uk

The Robert Gordon University
Schoolhill
Aberdeen
Scotland
AB10 1FR

Tel: 01224 26 27 28
Website: www.rgu.ac.uk

Roehampton University of Surrey
Whitelands College
West Hill
London
SW15 3SN

Tel: 020 8392 3232
Website: www.roehampton.ac.uk

Royal Academy of Dance
Faculty of Education
36 Battersea Square
SW11 3RA

Tel: 020 7326 8034/8049
Website: www.rad.org.uk

Royal Holloway, University of London
Egham
Surrey
TW20 0EX

Tel: 01784 434455
Website: www.rhul.ac.uk

Royal Veterinary College (University of
London)
Royal College Street
London
NW1 0TU

Tel: 020 7468 5148
Website: www.rvc.ac.uk

Royal Welsh College of Music and
Drama (Coleg Brenhinol Cerdd a
Drama Cymru)
Castle Grounds
Cathays Park
Cardiff
CF10 3ER

Tel: 029 2034 2854
Website: www.rwcmd.ac.uk

The University of Salford
Salford
M5 4WT

Tel: 0161 295 5000
Website: www.salford.ac.uk

School of Oriental and African Studies
(University of London)
Thornhaugh Street
Russell Square
London
WC1H 0XG

Tel: 020 7074 5106
Website: www.soas.ac.uk

The School of Pharmacy (University of
London)
29–39 Brunswick Square
London
WC1N 1AX

Tel: 020 7753 5831
Website: www.ulsop.ac.uk

The University of Sheffield
9 Northumberland Road
Sheffield
S10 2TT

Tel: 0114 222 2000
Website: www.sheffield.ac.uk

Sheffield Hallam University
City Campus
Howard Street
Sheffield
S1 1WB

Tel: 0114 225 5555
Website: www.shu.ac.uk

University of Southampton
Highfield
Southampton
SO17 1BJ

Tel: 023 8059 5000
Website: www.soton.ac.uk

Southampton Institute
East Park Terrace
Southampton
Hampshire
SO14 0RT

Tel: 023 8031 9000
Website: www.solent.ac.uk

University of St Andrews
Admissions Office
79 North Street
St Andrews
KY16 9AJ

Tel: 01334 462150
Website: www.st-andrews.ac.uk

St George's Hospital Medical School
(University of London)
Cranmer Terrace
London
SW17 0RE

Tel: 020 8725 5201/0499
Website: www.sghms.ac.uk

The College of St Mark and St John
Derriford Road
Plymouth
PL6 8BH

Tel: 01752 636890
Website: www.marjon.ac.uk

St Mary's University College
191 Falls Road
BT12 6FE

Tel: 028 9032 7678
Website: www.stmarys-belfast.ac.uk

Staffordshire University
College Road
Stoke on Trent
ST4 2DE

Tel: 01782 292753
Website: www.staffs.ac.uk

The University of Stirling
Stirling
FK9 4LA

Tel: 01786 467044
Website: www.stir.ac.uk

The University of Strathclyde
Glasgow
G1 1XQ

Tel: 0141 552 4400
Website: www.strath.ac.uk

University of Sunderland
Student Recruitment
Edinburgh Building
Chester Road
SR1 3SD

Tel: 0191 515 3000
Website: www.sunderland.ac.uk

University of Surrey
Stag Hill
Guildford
Surrey
GU2 7XH

Tel: 01483 689305
Website: www.surrey.ac.uk

The Surrey Institute of Art and Design
University College
Falkner Road
Farnham
Surrey
GU9 7DS

Tel: 01252 892696/09/10/11
Website: www.surrart.ac.uk

University of Sussex
Undergraduate Office (Admissions)
Sussex House
University of Sussex
BN1 9RH

Tel: 01273 678416
Website: www.sussex.ac.uk

Swansea, University of Wales
Singleton Park
Swansea
SA2 8PP

Tel: 01792 295111
Website: www.swansea.ac.uk

University of Teesside
Middlesbrough
TS1 3BA
Tel: 01642 218121
Website: www.tees.ac.uk

Thames Valley University
St Mary's Road
Ealing
London
W5 5RF

Tel: 0800 036 8888
Website: www.tvu.ac.uk

Trinity College Carmarthen
College Road
Carmarthen
SA31 3EP

Tel: 01267 676767
Website: www.trinity-cm.ac.uk

University of Ulster
Coleraine
Co. Londonderry
Northern Ireland
BT52 1SA

Tel: 028 7032 4221
Website: www.ulster.ac.uk

University College London (University
of London)
Gower Street
London
WC1E 6BT

Tel: 020 7679 3000
Website: www.ucl.ac.uk

University of Wales College of
Medicine
Heath Park
Cardiff
CF14 4XN

Tel: 029 2074 2027
Website: www.uwcm.ac.uk

The University of Warwick
Coventry
CV4 7AL

Tel: 024 7652 3723
Website: www.warwick.ac.uk

University of Westminster
115 New Cavendish Street
London
W1W 6UW

Tel: 020 7911 5000
Website: www.wmin.ac.uk

Wimbledon School of Art
Merton Hall Road
London
SW19 3QA

Tel: 020 8408 5000
Website: www.wimbledon.ac.uk

University of Wolverhampton
Admissions Unit
Compton Road West
Wolverhampton
WV3 9DX

Tel: 01902 321000
Website: www.wlv.ac.uk

University College Worcester
Henwick Grove
Worcester
WR2 6AJ

Tel: 01905 855111
Website: www.worc.ac.uk/worcs.html

Writtle College
Chelmsford
Essex
CM1 3RR

Tel: 01245 424200
Website: www.writtle.ac.uk

The University of York
Admissions and Schools Liaison
University of York
Heslington
YO10 5DD

Tel: 01904 433533/433539
Website: www.york.ac.uk